A Beginner's Guide to
Terrarium Gardening

Succulents · Air Plants · Cacti · Moss · And more!

Sueko Katsuji · Motoko Suzuki
Kazuto Kihara · Yuya Ohyama

TUTTLE Publishing

Tokyo | Rutland, Vermont | Singapore

CONTENTS

What is a Terrarium?

A terrarium is a small green space that is created in a transparent container consisting of various plants and other materials. As mini-gardens that can be enjoyed indoors by anyone, terrariums are becoming increasingly popular. The plants you can use range from air plants, which are easy even for beginners to handle, to mosses, succulents, cacti and more. The accessories or decorative materials that are used along with the plants are varied too, such as driftwood, stones and pebbles, sea shells and so on, which can be arranged in many ways. Completed terrariums can be used to brighten up your decor and they also make great gifts. We invite you to use the examples presented in this book as an inspiration for creating your own terrariums.

Basic Tools for Making Terrariums

Here are the tools that are handy to have when putting together a terrarium.
Be sure to have some tools on hand that are helpful for terrarium making
such as long tweezers, a funnel, and a brush.

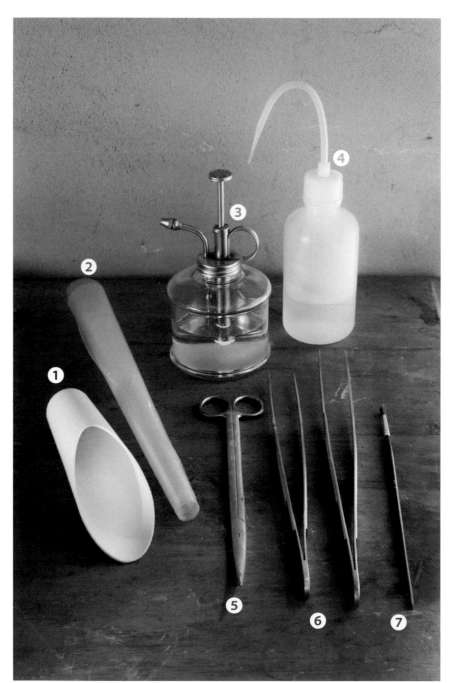

 Small scoop
Used to add soil or sand to the container. This is handy for filling containers with wide openings meant for succulents. Choose the most compact one you can find.

 Funnel
Used to place soil or sand into narrow spaces. If you use a clear file folder for this purpose, you can adjust how narrow it is when you roll it up.

③ Spray bottle
Used to water air plants and mosses evenly. The type that has a narrow spraying end that can be inserted into containers is recommended.

 Watering device
Used to water the roots of a plant directly as well as water succulents or cacti. It is recommended that you use one with a long nozzle that can be inserted into the container.

 Scissors
Used to maintain a terrarium by cutting the leaves of plants or trimming mosses. Scissors meant for use in acquariums are long and thin and easy to use.

⑥ Tweezers
Used to pick up materials and place them in the container or to arrange the layout of the terrarium. Choose the right size for the height and size of the container you're landscaping.

⑦ Brush
This is used to brush off any soil or dust on the container, or dirt on the plants. It's best to use a brush that is the right size for the container, but in any case a thin brush is easiest to use.

Basic Materials

The materials used to create a terrarium can be divided into ones that are needed for the plants to thrive and ones that are purely decorative which complement the plants. Choose the materials that go well with the plants you are using.

Materials Used for Planting

① Bark chips
Finely chipped tree bark is used mainly in combination with mosses, taking advantage of its superior water retaining ability.

② Succulent soil
A growing medium that is well suited for succulents. It usually contains a mixture of effective draining materials such as pumice stone and bark compost.

③ Sand
The sand shown here is La Plata, a river sand from Argentina. It is airy and drains well, and is great for use with air plants, succulents and cacti. There are many colors of sand from various regions around the world that you can also use.

④ Pine bark
Shredded pine bark is bouncy and retains water well, and is well suited for moss terrariums. Use with or instead of bark chips.

⑤ Aqua soil
Aqua soil is a growing medium for use in aquariums. Because it is very rich in nutrients and designed to absorb the debris in aquarium water, it is ideal for moss terrariums.

⑥ Zeolite aquarium substrate
Zeolite medium or aquarium substrate is made up mostly of crushed aluminosilicate minerals. It prevents plant roots from rotting, and provides a healthy growing environment. It's is airy and retains water well yet drains well too, and is an ideal material for terrariums.

Decorative Materials

① Curly moss
Dried moss that is long and curly. Usually comes in green or white.

② Iceland moss
Dried moss that has a curly, woolly appearance. It can be used as-is for decorative purposes or its water retaining qualities can be utilized for combining with living moss.

③ Wood chips
Finely chipped wood comes in a lot of colors and fragrances. Choose the ones that fit the mood and look you are after.

④ Coral sand
Coral sand is made from crushed coral. Recommended for use with air plants to create a cool, summery look.

⑤ Driftwood
Wood that has been floating in sea or freshwater. There is a wide variety of colors and shapes to choose from depending on the type of wood. Choose the pieces that fit the mood and look you are after.

⑥ Stones
Decorative stones come in numerous shapes and sizes, and are sold at most gardening stores. Great for creating a natural look.

⑦ Cork
Cork has a very distinct look. It can be used as a decorative touch to create very stylish terrariums.

⑧ Moss covered branches
Moss-covered branches are sold for use in bonsai. Combine with living mosses to create an elegant look.

Other Decorative Materials

Natural stones and crystals
There are many different natural stones and crystals you can use, from transparent to ones that are purple, green, smoky and more.

Coral, sea shells, nuts, etc.
These materials are especially useful for creating seasonal designs. For example, combine coral, seashells, and sand for a summery look.

Miniature figures
These tiny figures are used in dioramas. Fix them onto stones, branches or other materials with a glue gun.

Basic Instructions and Tips for Making Terrariums

Here we show you how to put together an air plant terrarium, a moss terrarium, and a succulent or cacti terrarium. Let's master the workflow of creating all kinds of terrariums.

1

Clean the container

A dirty container ruins the look of your creation. Before adding anything, make sure to wipe the container clean with a damp cloth.

2

Position large items first

A fundamental rule is to decide on the positions of large objects before you put them in the container. You should also put in the tall or voluminous plants first in order to create a well-balanced composition.

3

Tamp down each layer well

When you want to show off the layers of soil, sand, gravel and so on, make sure to tamp down each layer in the container very well with each addition so that they don't get crooked.

Make terrariums that can be enjoyed from multiple angles

Turn the container as you work and arrange the items within. Plants show many different faces depending on whether you look at them from above, diagonally, and so on.

4

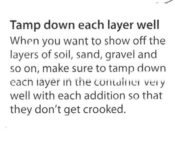

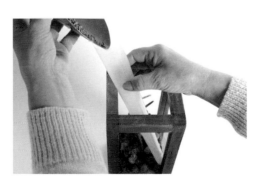

5

Adjust the area around the plants very carefully

When positioning thin or small plants, work very carefully so as not to damage them. When adding soil or other mediums, make the end of your funnel (see the Tools section) very narrow and add the medium a little at a time so that it does not hit the plant.

How to Make an Air Plant Terrarium

Air plant terrariums offer a lot of freedom since the plants don't need any soil to grow in.
Position the plants so that they can be taken out easily for watering.

1 Make the materials and plants (see page 29) ready. We will be using the wire that comes with the Spanish moss.

2 Using a small scoop, put coral sand into the container. The volcanic stone that is used in this example is very tall, so be sure not to add too much coral sand.

3 Position the stones in the middle. Add the larger stone first, then put in the smaller stone so that it is supporting the larger one.

4 Position the air plants—in this case Tillandsia bulbosa, Tillandsia butzii, Tillandsia funckiana and Tillandsia loliacea— in the indentions of the large stone.

5 Wrap the roots of the Tillandsia tectorum with wire, and cut off the ends, leaving them long as shown here.

6 Hook the ends of the wire wrapped around the Tillandsia tectorum in Step 5 onto the wire wrapped around the Spanish moss, and fix in place.

7 Hook the wire wrapped around the Tillandsia tectorum onto the container base.

8 Place the glass container on top of the base in Step 7, taking care not to crush the Tillandsia tectorum.

9 To create the other container, fill with coral sand as with the first container, and position the Banksia, then the Tillandsia xerographica in that order.

How to Make a Moss Terrarium

When you are creating a moss terrarium, make sure that the environment within the container can retain humidity. The key point is is to push the bark chip layer to the sides, so that you can see the layers.

1 Make the materials and plants ready (see page 33). Take the moss out of their sealed containers just before planting them to avoid drying them out.

2 Put zeolite in the bottom of the container using a scoop and tamp it down. Add bark chips on top of that layer, and push it to the sides.

3 Add Aqua soil using a funnel. Aim for the center, so that you do not disturb the bark chip layer added in Step 2.

4 Add the stones and moss covered branch to the container, making sure they are placed in a balanced manner.

5 Place the plants in this order. Selaginella remotifolia; Selaginella; Fissidens; Racomitrium japonicum or sunagoke moss; and Leucobryum bowringii Mitt. or mountain moss.

6 Use tweezers to poke the Aqua soil so that the roots are well buried in it. Tidy up the inside of the container.

7 Moisten a piece of wadded-up paper towel, hold it with the tweezers, and wipe off any dirt that has gotten onto the sides of the container.

8 To finish, mist everything in the container to set the plants in place.

9 Put a piece of wax paper on the mouth of the container and tie with a piece of hemp twine. A moss terrarium should be kept sealed with some kind of lid as much as possible.

How to Make a Succulent and Cactus Terrarium

Succulents and cacti should be planted in airy containers with large openings
and planted securely with their roots well covered.

1 Assemble the materials (see page 24). Succulents grow at different rates and in different seasons, so select varieties that have similar growing habits.

2 Pour zeolite into the bottom of the container and smooth out the surface by tamping it until it's flat.

3 Add succulent growing medium on top. Adjust the height of the growing medium depending on the height of the other materials.

4 Put the large pumice stone in the center.

5 Position the Seyrigia humbertii behind the stone using tweezers.

6 Position the Lithops (living stones) and Sempervivum (house leeks) in front of the stone with the tweezers. Be careful not to bury the tiny plants.

7 Using the funnel, add some succulent growing medium little by little to fill the gaps and to cover the roots of the plants.

8 Tamp down the soil by poking with the tweezers and make any adjustments if needed.

9 Fill a small container using the same steps. Add zeolite first, then succulent growing medium, stones and a kiwi vine, then plant the Sansevieria humbertiana and the Mammillaria pectinifera (Solisia pectinata) cactus.

How to Match Terrarium Containers with Contents

Terrariums are basically created by matching up the container with what goes inside, and this is where your creative sense comes into play. Let's look at the unique terrarium below which combines both design and function.

The Torch

The interior green design shop Pianta×Stanza (designed and operated by Ryokuensha Co.) aims to combine house plants with interior design to create new ways of looking at the spaces we inhabit. One of the items they have created using this concept is the Torch. The distinctive shape of the round container, which resembles an alcohol lamp, is enhanced by adding a flickering light, which makes it look like there's a flame inside. A rope beneath the kokedama (moss ball) nestled on top of the container draws water, so that the kokedama does not need to be watered frequently by hand. Not only does the Torch look good, its practical functionality has also drawn a lot of praise. Try challenging yourself to create playful terrariums like this one!

How to Care for Air Plants

Air plants are a group of plants called Tillandsia, in the Bromeliaceae family (the same as pineapples). They do not need any soil to grow and are characterized by their ability to absorb moisture from the air through their leaves and stems. The fine water-absorbing hairs on air plants are called Trichomes when the air is dry, these stand up to gather the the available moisture from the atmosphere. There are more than 600 varieties of air plants, which are roughly divided into two categories: silver leaf and green leaf. The leaves and stems of the silver leaf types are covered with trichomes while the green leaf types have few trichomes and do not stand dryness very well.

Examples of Air Plants

Tillandsia tectorum
The most popular type of air plant. The trichome covered leaves seem to sparkle. This is a perfect choice for the focus point of a terrarium.

Tillandsia caput medusae
This plant is characterized by dramatic twisting leaves and a bulbous lower part. It can add a fun touch to a terrarium.

Tillandsia bergeri
Tillandsia bergeri spreads its abundant strong, spiky leaves in a spiral pattern. This is a plant with lots of presence. It grows easily and propogates in clumps, so you can enjoy seeing it transform.

Containers

Choose a container that has a wide opening and is well ventilated. Because air plants aren't too picky about where they are placed, you can try hanging them, or even arrange them so they are sticking out of the container. That's the advantage of using air plants.

Watering

Once or twice a week, mist all the plants generously. In the winter you only need to do this once a week. Always take air plants out of the container before misting them, then shake off any excess water very well before returning them to the container. If you put them back while they are still wet, it will lead to mold and rot.

Placement

You can put an air plant terrarium anywhere you like, as long as it's not in direct sunlight. However, you should avoid putting the terrarium in deep shade, otherwise it may become too humid. Be careful not to let the inside of the container become too humid.

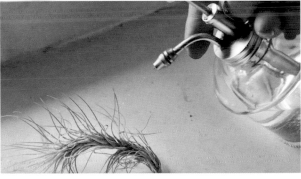

Maintenance

If you think a plant is looking unwell, mist it with liquid fertilizer diluted with water. Air plants don't like cold either, so make sure they are placed in the right temperature.

How to Care for Mosses

Mosses grow on old wood, in humid areas, on rocks and so forth. They dislike dryness, and prefer very humid, damp places. There are more than 2,000 varieties of moss in Japan alone, and it's estimated there are around 12,000 worldwide. Mosses do not flower or make seeds; they propagate by releasing spores. When a moss dries out, the surface becomes withered and it looks like it has died, but it's actually very tough. When you give a moss that looks dead plenty of water, more often than not it will come back to life, green and luscious. Hypnum plumaeforme and Leucobryum bowringii Mitt. or mountain moss can be found quite easily at garden centers and home centers; if you can't find them, try looking for similar mosses.

Examples of Mosses

Leucobryum juniperoideum (smaller white moss)
Also called mountain moss or steamed bun moss in Japan, this moss has a plump, cushiony look and soft, wavy "hair." It is relatively resistant to drought, and is easy for beginners to grow.

Rhodobryum (Schimp.) Hampe (big umbrella moss)
This moss looks like opened up leaves. Its small flower-like appearance is very popular. It can be used in terrariums with small openings.

Pogonatum contortum (contorted pogonatum moss)
This is a type of moss that is used in outdoor gardens as well as in terrariums, and is characterized by its straight stems that grow upwards. Try planting them in a long container so that you can enjoy watching them grow.

Containers

Choose a container with a lid or a small opening, so that it's easy to maintain the humidity inside. Alternatively, you can make a lid by sealing the opening with wax paper.

Watering

If the container is sealed, you just need to water the mosses every three to four days. Mist them generously with a spray bottle. If you have planted them together with succulents or cacti, be careful not to overwater.

Placement

Place the container in a location indoors which does not get direct sunlight. Although mosses do well out of sunlight, they will do better if you can put them in a place that does get some light during the day.

Maintenance

If you find parts that have gone brown, cut them off with scissors. New moss will grow again from there.

How to Care for Succulents

Succulents have thick leaves and stems that are filled with water. Since they mostly grow in dry, often hot climates such as deserts and coastlines, they grow well in low humidity, dry environments. Their cute, fresh and juicy plump appearance makes succulents a very popular plant, and they are often grown in groups. There are a huge variety of succulents, which can be divided into summer, winter and spring-fall types depending on when their growth periods are. When you plant them together, be sure to choose varieties that have the same growth period. Although this depends on each variety, in general succulents should be replanted every 1 to 2 years.

Examples of Succulent Plants

Haworthias
Some haworthias have leaves that are stiff and pointy leaves and others that are soft and translucent. The one in this photo is a Haworthia obtusa, which has soft semi-transparent tips. Arrange it so the patterns on the leaves are visible.

Senecios
Senecios stand out because of their wonderfully strange and interesting leaves, which come in many shapes. The one here is a Senecio serpens (also called a Curio serpens). It has beautifully plump, long and elongated leaves that have a dusty white hue.

Aeoniums
Aeoniums, or tree houseleeks, are characterized by stems that grow straight up. By combining them with kokedama (moss balls), you can emphasize their pretty flower-like shapes.

Containers

Select containers that have large openings and are well ventilated. If they like their environment, succulents can grow to be quite large, so try to choose a container with plenty of space for them to grow.

Watering

Succulents grow in dry climates, so be sure not to overwater them. Keep their natural growing seasons in mind and water them once or twice a week during that growing period. Use a watering device with a nozzle, aiming directly at the roots. When they aren't in their active growing periods, you can just water them about once every two weeks. If water pools inside the container, the roots may rot, so soak them up thoroughly.

Placement

Place in a bright, sunny location indoors with good air flow. Avoid direct sunlight. Winter-type succulents especially dislike high temperatures and humidity, so be careful not to let heat build up within the container.

Maintenance

The leaves of succulents may turn brown due to temperature fluctuations. You just need to cut off any brown parts that you see with scissors. Transplant them during their respective growing periods. You can propagate them when transplanting if any pups or small child plants have grown around them. Just take the pups off and plant them on their own.

How to Care for Cacti

Cacti, or cactuses, belong to the plant family Cactaceae, and almost all have succulent, water-filled leaves and stems. Although classification varies by method, it's said that there are more than 2,000 varieties of cacti. Because they withstand heat well and don't need much watering, they are ideal plants for beginners.

The main difference between cacti and succulents is that the former have areoles, small bumps from which spines grow, sometimes with a cotton wool-like fluff. Although there are some cactus varieties with no thorns, all cacti have areoles. Cactus spines are very sharp and you may hurt yourself if you handle them with your bare hands. Use long tweezers to plant them in terrariums.

Containers
Cacti basically have the same growing requirements as succulents, so select containers with large openings that have good air circulation around the plants. If you are using a container with a lid, make sure to open it occasionally to ventilate it.

Placement
Avoid direct sunlight and position cactus terrariums in a bright, well ventilated place indoors. Be especially careful of humidity buildup inside the container if you live in a humid climate or on rainy days.

Watering
Water cacti just once every 1–2 weeks, whenever the planting material is dried out. Use a syringe or a watering device with a nozzle to aim the water directly at the roots and avoid wetting the plant itself.

How to Care for Other Plants

House plants that can be combined with the previous plant types mentioned are recommended for terrariums too. The growing conditions required by house plants vary a lot, but generally speaking many are quite easy to take care of, even for beginners. In this book we have combined ferns with mosses, which both prefer moist conditions and grow on wood, and we've also made the colorful, pretty flowers of Cryptanthus the main feature in a terrarium. Have fun experimenting with the house plants you can find easily at garden or home centers, and arranging them in your terrariums.

Cryptanthus

The leaves of this plant grow in a distinct, star-shaped pattern. Enhance its bright colors by using materials with muted tones with it, so that the plant becomes the star of your creation.

Davallia tyermanii (bear's paw fern, white rabbit's foot fern)

This is a tropical fern that has serrated leaves that grow upwards, with a fluffy fur covering the rhizotamous roots. Although it's an epiphyte (a plant that grows on other plant material), it can be planted in moist soil too, so feel free to combine it with mosses.

Muehlenbeckia (wire plant)

The creeping variety of this plant (also called wire vine) is called Muehlenbeckia axillaris. The wire plant has many thin, wire-like vines, and lots of volume. It's an ideal plant to use as an accent in a terrarium.

Terrarium FAQs

Here we answer some of the most commonly asked questions about terrariums.
Please refer to these pages when you get stuck.

Q

How many years can a terrarium last?

A

Although this depends on the types of plants in it, you can typical enjoy a terrarium for 1 to 2 years. If the plants stay healthy, a terrarium can be kept alive for even longer. If the plants grow too big for the container and no longer fit, you can try cutting them back, dividing or replanting them. All this depends on the container you select and where you position them, so try to use a combination of factors that is optimal for the plants you use.

Q

What plants are recommended for terrarium beginners?

A

When you are making a terrarium for the first time, air plants, which do not need to be planted in a medium or soil, are the easiest to handle. They aren't at all picky about the materials they are combined with, and can fit easily into any design. There are many varieties of air plants from which you can choose. They're also really easy to take care of, since you only need to mist them about once or twice a week, which accounts for their popularity.

Q

Where can I find terrarium containers?

A

Many garden centers as well as interior design stores sell glass containers for terrariums these days. These include multi-sided containers that show off the contents, as well as hanging containers. You can of course buy a container specifically meant for terrrariums, but you can also use anything you have on hand such as a glass flower vase, a jar, and so on.

Q

What should I do if the plants get sick?

A

If you think your plants don't look too well, observe them carefully to determine the cause. Sometimes plants get damaged due to temperature changes and wither. In that case, you just need to remove any dead leaves. If the leaves or stems are discolored or rotting, check the roots. If they have turned black, remove the plant.

Q
Can I put a terrarium outdoors?

A

Terrariums basically do best when placed indoors out of direct sunlight. Depending on the type of plants inside, even a sunny windowsill can be too much and the plants may suffer. Terrariums with air plants, succulents or cacti can be placed in an well ventilated location in the shade outdoors, but the temperature inside the container can build up quite a bit in the summer, so it's best to bring the container indoors in the hot months.

Q
Can I gather my own moss in the wild?

A

Moss grows all over the place in the wild in humid climates, so you can find and gather it in the wild yourself. However, you need to make sure you are allowed to gather moss in a particular location beforehand, and that the moss you are taken is not a protected variety. Even in public areas, often moss gathering is prohibited by law. When gathering moss, use a spatula or a hand trowel to scoop it up gently, and take it home in a covered plastic container.

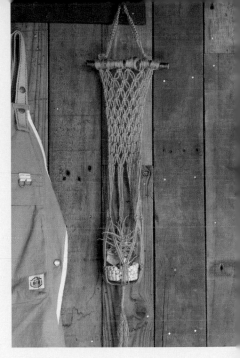

Q
What materials are suitable for use in terrariums?

A

When you want to create a naturalistic design, use natural materials such as driftwood, stones and pebbles, sand and so on. When you want to do something a bit different, try anything that appeals to you such as bits of newspaper. To create a seasonal feel, use sea shells and coral in the summer, or dry branches and dried cotton flowers and in the winter. You can also have fun adding miniature figures to create stories within your containers too.

Q
How can I create a terrarium as a gift?

A

Terrariums are very popular as presents for anniversaries, or any special occasion. When creating a terrarium as a gift, use plants that are easy to care for such as air plants and mosses. Including flowering plants like Tillandsia ionantha is sure to be a hit too. Don't forget to gift wrap the terrarium. Besides using paper, you can put the terrarium in a special box, or wrap it in clear cellophane and tie it with a bow so the contents are visible.

21

A Hanging Terrarium with Devil's Trumpets

Sueko Katsuji | Buriki no Zyoro

Simple hanging cylindrical containers contain Tillandsia air plants and soft, gentle curly moss contrasting with the spiky round shapes of Datura metal seed capsules. The contrasting textures of the dried plant material is a perfect foil for the green of the tillandsias.

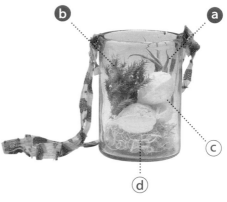

Plants
ⓐ Tillandsia caput-medusae (air plant)
ⓑ Tillandsia tricholepis (air plant)

Materials
ⓒ Datura metal or devil's trumpet (dried seed capsules)
ⓓ Curly moss (dried)

Container
Outer diameter: 4½" (12 cm)
Height: 6⅔" (17 cm)

Instructions
1. Line the bottom of the container with a fluffy layer of curly moss.
2. Stack up 3 datura capsules to add height.
3. Position the Tillandsia tricholepis and the Tillandsia caput-medusae, in that order.

Creation/Care Tips
Combine air plants with dried flower elements for a terrarium with a playful feel. The spiky seed capsules of the Datura metal are very distinctive.

A Wild Landscape of Mosses, Stones and Ferns

Sueko Katsuji | Buriki no Zyoro

Five types of mosses are laid out in a compact glass jar. In order to avoid it becoming too crowded and messy looking, stones and twigs are added judiciously as accents. Using pine tree bark and bark chips is another good way of balancing out the landscape within the jar.

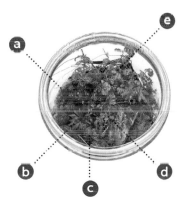

Plants
a Leucobryum bowringii Mitt. (moss)
b Rhodobryum (Schimp). Hampe (moss)
c Pogonatum contortum or contorted pogonatum moss (moss)
d Racomitrium japonicum or sunagoke (moss)
e Selaginella remotifolia (fern)

Materials
(f) Stone
(g) Twig
(h) Aqua soil
(i) Pine bark
(j) Bark chips
(k) Zeolite

Container
Outer diameter: 5½″ (14 cm)
Height: 7⅞″ (20 cm)

Instructions
1. Put enough zeolite in to cover the bottom of the jar.
2. Put the bark chips and pine bark in the bottom and on the sides of the jar.
3. Add Aqua soil to the center of the jar.
4. Arrange the stones and twigs in a well balanced way.
5. Put in the **e** fern, then add the mosses in this order: **c**, **b**, **d** and **a**.

Creation/Care Tips
If you put a lot of plants in a small container, it will inevitably get crowded as they grow. Keep trimming them back to keep them looking attractive.

Terrariums Framed in Wooden Cases

Sueko Katsuji | Buriki no Zyoro

Glass cases framed with wood make any plant look stylish. Because they are easy to handle, you can place them anywhere. Here two cases are used in different sizes, each with similarly themed terrariums inside and displayed side to side. The succulents and cacti peeking out of the generous amount of soil are very cute and seen together they look like framed pictures.

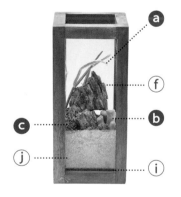

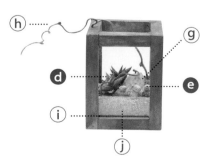

Plants
ⓐ Seyrigia humbertii (succulent)
ⓑ Lithops or living stone (succulent, variety unknown)
ⓒ Sempervivum or house leek (succulent, variety unknown)
ⓓ Sansevieria humbertiana (succulent)
ⓔ Mammillaria pectinifera (cactus)

Materials
ⓕ Pumice stone
ⓖ Stone
ⓗ Kiwi vine
ⓘ Zeolite
ⓙ Succulent growing soil/medium

Container
Tall
About 5" (13 cm) x 5" (13 cm) x 10¼" (26 cm)
Small
About 5" (13 cm) x 5" (13 cm) x 6¼" (16 cm)

Instructions on page 10.

Creation/Care Tips
Keep the terrariums out of direct sunlight. Water about once every two weeks, aiming the water directly at the roots and trying not to make the leaves wet.

Delicate Rose Moss and Bark Chips in a Flask

Sueko Katsuji | Buriki no Zyoro

Although flasks are associated with lab experiments, they make very attractive terrarium containers. The bright green Rhodobryum giganteum (rose moss) may look quite plain, but as its Japanese name "Umbrella Moss" indicates, the leaves look like open umbrellas and are very pretty. Try placing this terrarium in your bedroom or study, somewhere where you want to relax.

Plants
ⓐ Rhodobryum giganteum (moss)

Materials
ⓑ Aqua soil
ⓒ Bark chips
ⓓ Zeolite

Instructions
1. Put in enough zeolite to cover the bottom of the flask.
2. Add about ⅓ inch (1 cm) of bark chips.
3. Pour in Aqua soil, aiming for the center as much as possible.
4. Plant the moss into the Aqua soil using tweezers.

Creation/Care Tips
Make sure to plant the Rhodobryum giganteum moss roots firmly into the Aqua soil.

A Stylish Terrarium with Dried Flowers and Succulents

Sueko Katsuji | Buriki no Zyoro

A bouquet that combines both dried plants and succulents is enclosed in a simple glass container for a refined, distinct look. The texture of succulents matches well with wild dried plants, so by combining them you can achieve some dramatic effects. The key is to vary the height of the plants to create an interesting shape.

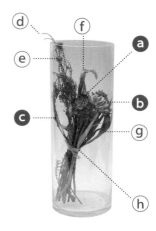

Plants
ⓐ Echeveria "Mebina" with a grafted branch of Kalanchoe daigremontiana "fushicho" (succulent)
ⓑ Echeveria runyonii "Topsy Turvy" (succulent)
ⓒ Disocactus anguliger or fishbone cactus (cactus)

Materials
ⓓ Grevillea "Ivanhoe" or spider flower (dried flowers)
ⓔ Leucadendron "jade pearl" (dried flowers)
ⓕ Saracenia or trumpet pitchers (dried flowers)
ⓖ Grevillea baileyana or white oak (dried flowers)
ⓗ Hemp twine

Container
Outer diameter: 6" (15 cm)
Height: 15¾" (40 cm)

Instructions
1. Gather the succulents, cactus and dried flowers together in a bouquet.
2. Tie with the twine, and put into the container.

Creation/Care Tips
When grafting a branch or stem onto another plant, make sure to do it on a plant from the same family. In this case both echeverias and kalanchoes are in the Crassulaceae family. Kalanchoe daigremontiana "fushicho" grows fast, so when a stem reaches the right length, cut off the leaves and use as the graft. Cut the end of the stem diagonally to expose a large surface and tie it securely to the plant you want to graft it onto. Grafts should be done when the plants are in their growing season.

Charming Air Plants with Twine and a News Clipping

Sueko Katsuji | Buriki no Zyoro

Your eye is drawn to the Tillandsia baileyi "Halley's Comet" first in this rounded flower vase. If you arrange the air plants to emphasize their different heights, the entire landscape will come to life. Add even more character and take the design to another level with hemp twine and a decorative piece of newspaper.

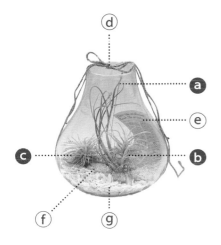

Plants
ⓐ Tillandsia baileyi "Halley's Comet" (air plant)
ⓑ Tillandsia paleacea major (air plant)
ⓒ Tillandsia tectorum (air plant)

Materials
ⓓ Hemp twine
ⓔ Cut newspaper (one in a language you don't read looks more interesting than one from your local paper)
ⓕ Coral
ⓖ Wood chips (white)

Container
Outer diameter: about 9½" (24 cm)
Height: 10¼" (26 cm)

Instructions
1. Put wood chips in the bottom of the container.
2. Position the coral.
3. Plant the tillandsias in the order they are listed.
4. Add a piece of newspaper as a decoration.
5. Wrap and tie the twine around the containers.

Creation/Care Tips
Because of the container's narrow mouth and wide, bottom heavy shape, if you leave it in direct sunlight the temperature inside may become too high, so be careful.

A Small Sealed Bottle Terrarium

Sueko Katsuji | Buriki no Zyoro

Terrariums in small bottles can be hung near a window, placed on bookshelves and more. They are a great way to add a little something extra to your interior decor. Place the Pogonatum cirratum so that it is leaning against the side of the bottle, and adjust the branches so that each one is just a bit different in height, to give the plant an elegant presence.

Instructions

1. Put in enough zeolite to cover the bottom of the container.
2. Add a little Iceland moss.
3. Pour in about ⅓ inch (1 cm) of bark chips.
4. Add about 1⅓ inches (3 cm) of Aqua soil.
5. Plant the moss plants in the order listed.
6. Put on the bottle stopper, pass the twine through it, and hang the bottle up.

Creation/Care Tips

When the container you are using for your terrarium has a narrow opening, using long wire and tweezers makes planting easier.

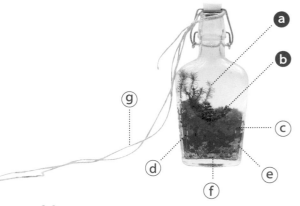

Plants

a Pogonatum cirratum (moss)
b Leucobryum neilgherrense C. Muell or Leucobryum juniperoideum (mountain moss)

Materials

ⓒ Aqua soil
ⓓ Bark chips
ⓔ Iceland moss (dried)
ⓕ Zeolite
ⓖ Hemp twine

Container

About 3" (8 cm) W x 1" (3 cm) D x 9" (23 cm) H

Dramatic Air Plant Terrariums on Iron Bases

Sueko Katsuji | Buriki no Zyoro

Distinctive containers with rusted iron bases are filled with a dramatic arrangement of materials. If you match the rugged stone with tillsandrias that have thin, delicate leaves, and the long banksia with thicker-leaved ones, each element will balance each other out well. Trail some Spanish moss under the container for an even more dramatic look.

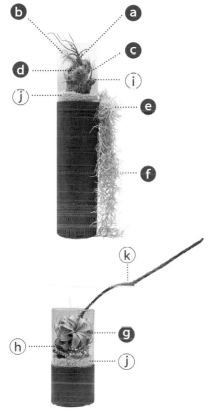

Plants
ⓐ Tillandsia bulbosa (air plant)
ⓑ Tillandsia funckiana (air plant)
ⓒ Tillandsia butzii (air plant)
ⓓ Tillandsia loliacea—a clump (air plant)
ⓔ Tillandsia tectorum (air plant)
ⓕ Tillandsia tectorum (air plant)
ⓖ Tillandsia xerographica or Spanish moss (air plant)

Materials
ⓗ Banksia (dried)
ⓘ Pumice stone
ⓙ Coral sand (fine)
ⓚ Branch

Containers
Tall container
Outer diameter: 6" (15 cm)
Height: 25½" (65 cm)

Small container
Outer diameter: 6" (15 cm)
Height: 12¾" (32.5 cm)

Instructions on page 8.

Creation/Care Tips
When you use non-plant materials in a dramatic way, the design can easily become unbalanced. To avoid this, put the materials in first, and then choose the right plants for the space.

Multi-Species Terrarium in a Stylish Jar

Sueko Katsuji | Buriki no Zyoro

Distinctive succulents, cacti and and an air plant are arranged together in this expressive terrarium. The container is chosen for its interesting and fun design. The pink and purple tinged leaves of the Haworthia cooperi give a warm, soft feeling.

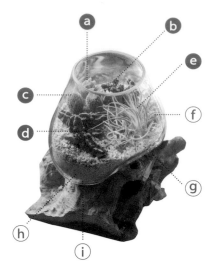

Plants

a Haworthia cooperi (succulent)
b Euphorbia grandicornis (succulent)
c Echinocereus rigidissimus (rainbow cactus)
d Echinocereus pentalophus cv. momotarou (ladyfinger cactus)
e Tillandsia kolbii (air plant)

Materials

f Branch (dry)
g Coral sand
h La Plata sand from Argentina
i Zeolite

Container

About 9½" (24 cm) W x 7" (18 cm) D x 9" (23 cm) H

Instructions

1. Put in enough zeolite to cover the bottom of the container.
2. Add a little La Planta sand.
3. Position the branch.
4. Add the first 4 plants listed in that order in a well-balanced arrangement.
5. Position the Tillandsia kolbii in an empty space.
6. Add coral sand around the plants to fix them into place.

Creation/Care Tips

Succulents and cacti do not have the same watering needs as air plants. To water the air plant, take it out of the container first.

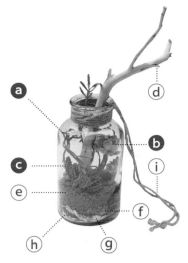

Plants
a Rhipsalis Ewaldiana (Mistletoe cactus)
b Mammillaria bombycina (silken pincushion cactus)
c Huernia brevirostris (succulent)

Materials
(d) Driftwood
(e) Succulent growing soil or medium
(f) Iceland moss (dried)
(g) Wood chips (white)
(h) Zeolite
(i) Hemp twine

Container
Outer diameter: 4" (10 cm)
Height: 8" (20 cm)

Instructions
1. Put the zeolite in the bottom of the container.
2. Add about ⅓ inch (1 cm) of wood chips.
3. Put in a ⅓ inch (1 cm) layer of Iceland moss.
4. Put the plants in in the order listed and plant them.
5. Pour in some succulent medium using a funnel around the plants and tamp it down carefully.
6. Position the driftwood.
7. Wrap the twine around the bottle several times, and hang it up.

Creation/Care Tips
If you plan to add the driftwood after you have put in the plants, make sure you leave enough space for it.

A Simple Hanging Terrarium with Driftwood
Sueko Katsuji | Buriki no Zyoro

When making a terrarium in a simple hanging bottle, try challenging yourself to create a design with lots of movement. The key to this design is the dynamic shapes of the Rhipsalis Ewaldiana and the driftwood. This lively terrararium with driftwood rising out of it is sure to brighten up any space.

Tillandsia and Cut Branches in an Artistic Frame

Sueko Katsuji | Buriki no Zyoro

The wood-framed showcase container and thick branches give this terrarium lots of presence. The star of the show is a Tillandsia caput-medusae, which got its name from the Greek mythological creature Medusa, whose snake-hair the leaves are thought to resemble. It is positioned in a way that creates an illusion of movement, to make it look as though it is fighting the branches.

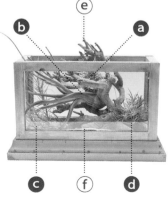

Plants
ⓐ Tillandsia chusgonensis (air plant)
ⓑ Tillandsia caput-medusae (air plant)
ⓒ Tillandsia caerulea (air plant)
ⓓ Tillandsia ionantha Fuego (air plant)

Materials
ⓔ Cut branches
ⓕ La Planta sand

Container
About 16" (41 cm) W x 8¼" (21 cm) D x 10" (25 cm) H

Instructions
1. Line the bottom of the container with La Planta sand. The key is to give the surface some hills and valleys instead of flattening it evenly.
2. Place the branch in a well-balanced way.
3. Add the Tillandsia caput-medusae, then the Tillandsia caerulea, followed by the Tillandsia ionantha Fuego and finally the Tillandsia chusgonensis.

Creation/Care Tips
Place the large wood piece first, then add the air plants in between the branches.

A Forest Floor with Branches, Ferns and Moss

Sueko Katsuji | Buriki no Zyoro

Planted with 5 different types of mosses and ferns that all have distinctive characteristics, this is a terrarium that is full of life. By adding some moss-covered branches and stones, it looks as if it were cut right out of a forest scene. If you want to enjoy this terrarium daily and take care of the plants, we recommend placing it on a window sill or another place that you will frequently pass.

Plants
a Selaginella (fern)
b Selaginella remotifolia (fern)
c Fissidens japonicus Doz. et Molk. (moss)
d Leucobryum juniperoidum (smaller white moss)
e Racomitrium japonicum (sunagoke moss)

Materials
f Moss covered branch
g Stone
h Aqua soil
i Bark chips
j Zeolite
k Waxed paper
l Hemp twine

Container
Outer diameter: 6¼" (16 cm)
Height: 12" (31 cm)

Instructions on page 9.

Creation/Care Tips
Cover the opening of the jar with wax paper to keep in the humidity. If any of the leaves go brown, cut them off with scissors and new leaves will grow from there.

A Small Greenhouse with Verdant Ferns and Moss

Sueko Katsuji | Buriki no Zyoro

This is a house-shaped terrarium that you could put somewhere it's easily seen like an entryway or living room. If you examine the unique looks of each moss or fern you choose, such as the variety of shapes and how green the leaves are, and place each one thoughtfully, you can create a dreamlike landscape within that compliments the eye-catching shape of the container. Use items like branches and stones to create a bold arrangement.

Plants
a Leucobryum juniperoidum (smaller white moss)
b Selaginella remotifolia (fern)
c Selaginella (fern)
d Nephrolepis cordifolia (fern)
e Adiantum peruvianum (fern)

Materials
f Moss-covered branch
g Coral stone
h Aqua soil
i Zeolite

Container
About 12″ (30 cm) W x 13″ (32 cm) D x 13″ (32 cm) H

Instructions
1. Place the coral stones so that they are distributed in a balanced manner.
2. Add enough zeolite to cover the bottom of the container.
3. Add about 2 inches (5 cm) of Aqua soil.
4. Place the moss-covered branch.
5. Put in the plants in this order: **b**, **d**, **e**, **c** and **a**.

Creation/Care Tips
The key to landscaping a large container as a terrarium is how you use the non-plant materials. Use the stones and branches wisely, as if you were creating a small landscape, then fill in between them with the plants. Consider the shapes and colors of the leaves as you arrange the plants.

Striking Vintage Container with Cacti and Succulents

Sueko Katsuji | Buriki no Zyoro

Cacti and succulents work really well in vintage-style containers. Emphasize the shapes of each plant to create this rather wild-looking terrarium. Since it's simple to take care of, you can enjoy it throughout your living space.

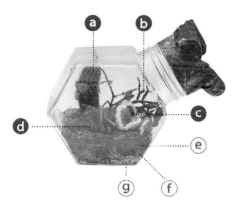

Plants

ⓐ Cosmopsis x "kaseiryu" (cactus)
ⓑ Rhipsalis burchellii (Mistletoe cactus)
ⓒ AustrocylIndropuntia vestita f. cristata (cactus)
ⓓ Echeveria "Black Knight" (succulent)

Materials

ⓔ Succulent soil or medium
ⓕ Iceland moss (dry)
ⓖ Zeolite

Container

9" (23 cm) W x 4¾" (12 cm) D x 7" (18 cm) H

Instructions

1. Put in enough zeolite to cover the bottom of the container.
2. Line with a layer of Iceland moss.
3. Position the plants in this order: **ⓐ**, **ⓒ**, **ⓑ**, then **ⓓ**.
4. Add succulent growing soil or medium around the plants, and settle them in.

Creation/Care Tips

Keep the terrarium out of direct sunlight and be careful of moisture buildup. After watering, leave the lid open for a while to air out the container.

A Desert Landscape of Cacti and Succulents

Motoko Suzuki | Tokyo Fantastic Omotesando

A fun collection of cacti that looks like a box of sweet treats. Pack in a lot of different plants in the square container for a festive, colorful look. Add natural, unpolished stones in various colors in the spaces left over, to create a rhythm of color and shape.

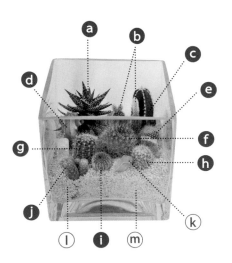

Plants
(a) Aloe descoingsii x haworthioides (succulent)
(b) Opuntia microdasys (bunny cactus)
(c) Pachycereus (cactus)
(d) Myrtillocactus geometrizans (blue-myrtle cactus)
(e) Echinocactus grusonii (yellow barrel cactus)
(f) Mammillaria spinosissima ("nishikimaru" cactus)
(g) Lobivia (cactus, variety unknown)
(h) Mammillaria fuauxiana (cactus)
(i) Parodia leninghausii (golden ball cactus)
(j) Mammillaria elongata (golden lace cactus)

Materials
(k) Natural stones (quartz, amethyst, fluorite, calcite)
(l) Zeolite
(m) White gravel

Container
4¾" (12 cm) square

Instructions
1. Put the gravel in the bottom of the container.
2. Arrange the cacti, starting with the largest ones, and going in size order.
3. Position the natural stones in between the cacti.
4. Slowly and carefully pour the zeolite around the plants, using a funnel.

Creation/Care Tips
Be careful not to tip over any of the numerous cacti when you pour in the zeolite.

Octagonal Hanging Terrariums with Colorful Moon Cacti

Motoko Suzuki | Tokyo Fantastic Omotesando

These octagonal hanging terrariums are filled with red and yellow moon cacti that contrast with the cute dots and stripes on the containers. Moon cacti are also called "candle cacti." Try these as hanging ornaments in a kitchen or living room.

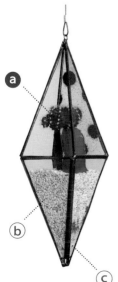

Plant

(a) Moon cacti (Gymnocalycium mihanovichii grafted onto hylocereus cacti)

Materials

(b) Zeolite

(c) Gravel (white, medium coarseness)

Container

3" (8 cm) W x 11½" (29 cm) H

Instructions

1. Put the gravel in the bottom of the container.
2. Position the cactus.
3. Pour zeolite slowly and carefully around the cactus using a funnel.

Creation/Care Tips

Either hang the container up or put it into a heavy container that can hold it securely in place while working on it.

An Overflowing Succulent Terrarium for Hanging

Motoko Suzuki | Tokyo Fantastic Omotesando

A pretty hanging terrarium that looks a little like soap bubbles swaying gently in the breeze. Plant the hanging Senecio rowleyanus (string of pearls) succulent so that it looks like it's spilling out of the container for a breezy, cool look. Accessorize the terrarium with sea shells in the summer and nuts or acorns in the fall to create a seasonal design.

Plants
a Sedum adolphi (succulent)
b Pachyphytum oviferum (moonstones, succulent)
c Sempervivum (houseleek, succulent)
d Rhipsalis (succulent)
e Senecio rowleyanus (string of pearls, succulent)

Materials
f Leather cord
g Nelsol succulent growing medium
Note Nelsol is a growing medium that can be mixed with water and formed into pellets. If you can't find it in your area, use clay pellets or another succulent growing medium instead.

Container:
Diameter: 4" (10 cm)

Instructions
1. If using Nelsol, add water to it and knead it like clay or dough.
2. Form pellets with the kneaded Nelsol, and put them in a flat layer in the container.
3. Arrange the plants.
4. Add more Nelsol pellets a little at a time around the plants.
5. Pass a leather cord through the upper part of the container and hang up to display.

Modern Angled Containers with Cacti and Air Plants

Motoko Suzuki | Tokyo Fantastic Omotesando

Two multi-angled containers, one large and one small, are displayed together, created as distinct but similarly-themed terrariums. They flow together to create an a fun look. By putting low-growing plants in the smaller container, which is positioned to the front, and taller plants and objects in the larger one, the sloping "ground" is emphasized and is beautifully matched. Let the plants in the foreground spill out a bit to expand the landscape even more.

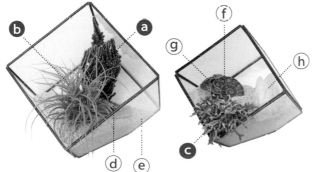

Plants
a Cereus (cactus)
b Tillandsia bergeri (air plant)
c Rhipsalis (cactus)

Materials
d Driftwood
e Zeolite
f Fossil stone (ammonite)
g Natural stone (half-cut agate)
h Natural stone (quartz)

Containers
Large
8½" (21.5 cm) W x 9½" (24 cm) H
Small
6" (15 cm) W x 7⅞" (20 cm) H

Instructions
Large container
1. Position the cereus cactus.
2. Pour the zeolite in slowly and carefully.
3. Position the tillandsia and driftwood.
Small container
1. Pour zeolite into the container.
2. Position the rhypsalis and natural stones.

Creation/Care Tips
Be careful not to add too much zeolite, and make sure it doesn't spill out of the container.

A Summertime Riverine Scene

Motoko Suzuki | Tokyo Fantastic Omotesando

Two footed containers, one large and one small, are filled with breezy air plants and mosses, and displayed together to depict a summertime riverbed scene. The more they grow, the more festive the abundant vines and tiny leaves of wire plants look, brightening the space they occupy.

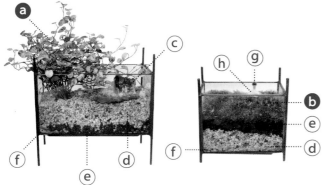

Plants
ⓐ Muehlenbeckia axillaris (wire plant)
ⓑ Leucobryum juniperoideum (smaller white moss)

Materials
ⓒ Natural stone (amethyst)
ⓓ Zeolite
ⓔ Potted plant soil or medium
ⓕ Gravel (medium, gray)
ⓖ Miniature figures
ⓗ Gravel (medium, white)

Containers
Large container
6" (15 cm) W x 3" (7.5 cm) D x 6" (15 cm) H
Small container
4" (10 cm) W x 2.5" (5.5 cm) D x 4" (10 cm) H

Instructions
Large container
1. Put the gravel in the bottom of the container.
2. Position the wire plants, and add the potting soil (medium).
3. Put in the stone.

Small container
1. Put the gravel in the bottom of the container.
2. Pour the zeolite in gently, then the potting soil (medium).
3. Put in the moss.
4. Attach the minature figures to the stones with a glue gun or instant glue. Position the stones.

Square Terrarium Dense with Succulents

Motoko Suzuki | Tokyo Fantastic Omotesando

A refreshing green collection of succulents that looks like a salad. Arrange the plants that grow vertically like the Kalanchoe marnieriana and Sedum allantoides in the back, make the showy Echeveria prelinze the central focus, and fill the foreground with the trailing string of pearls plant for a cohesive design.

Plants

- **a** Kalanchoe marnieriana (succulent, called "dance of the white princess")
- **b** Sedum allantoides (succulent)
- **c** Aeonium (succulent, also known as tree houseleek; called "pixie forest")
- **d** Cotyledon tomentosa (succulent, called "baby bear")
- **e** Echeveria prelinze (succulent)
- **f** Senecio rowleyanus (succulents, also known as string of pearl plant)

Materials

- **g** Zeolite
- **h** Gravel (fine, white)

Container

4¾" (12 cm) square

Instructions

1. Put the gravel in the bottom of the container.
2. Position the plants.
3. Gently pour in the zeolite.

Cacti in Mason Jars

Motoko Suzuki | Tokyo Fantastic Omotesando

These mason jars have lights inside them which spotlight the cacti within for a dramatic look. For containers like mason jars, which are mainly observed from the side, using plants with varying heights makes them more picturesque. Arrange natural stones in the gaps to balance the designs.

Plants
ⓐ Marginatocereus marginatus (cactus)
ⓑ Mammillaria marksiana (cactus)
ⓒ Gymnocalycium mihanovichii var. friedrichi "Hibotan" (redcap cactus)

Materials
ⓓ Natural stone (florite)
ⓔ Zeolite
ⓕ Gravel (medium, white)
ⓖ Coral
ⓗ Preserved moss (dried)

Containers
Large container
Outer diameter: 3½" (9 cm)
Height: 6⅔" (17 cm)
Small container
Outer diameter: 3⅓" (8.5 cm)
Height: 5½" (14 cm) high

Instructions
1. Put about ⅓ inch (1 cm) of gravel in the bottom of the jar.
2. Add zeolite to reach halfway up the jar.
3. Position the shorter cacti first, and add more zeolite to create a slope.
4. Arrange the stone, coral and preserved moss.

Creation/Care Tips
Turn the lights on at night for a stylish ambience. When cacti are lit up, they appear to give off a warm, relaxing glow. When the jars aren't lit, leave the lids open so that they get as much air as possible.

Succulents in an Airy Jewel Box

Motoko Suzuki | Tokyo Fantastic Omotesando

This terrarium combines Haworthia obtusa, which looks like a collection of small, semi-translucent shiny stones, and red-tinged Sedum rubrotinctum (jelly bean plant) to create a terrarium that looks like a jewelry box. Put it in an airy location to enjoy the way the light plays on these pretty plants.

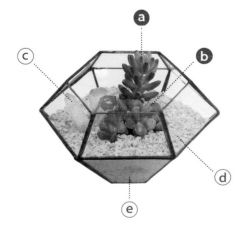

Plants
a Sedum rubrotinctum (succulent, also known as jelly bean plant)
b Haworthia obtusa (succulent)

Materials
c Natural stone (lemurian seed quartz)
d Zeolite
e Gravel (fine, white)

Container
5" W x 3" H (13 cm W x 8 cm H)

Instructions
1. Put gravel in the bottom of the container.
2. Position the succulents and gently pour in the zeolite.
3. Arrange the natural stone.

Creation/Care Tips
Position the taller plant in the back for better balance. It's a good idea to plan where the crystal should go before you position the plants.

Angled Containers with Succulents and Seashells

Motoko Suzuki | Tokyo Fantastic Omotesando

These elegant stained glass footed trapezoidal containers are filled with colorful succulents, white quartz and a sea shell to evoke a beach scene. Display them in a well-lit place to emphasize the blue and yellow colors created by the glass, as well as the summery design.

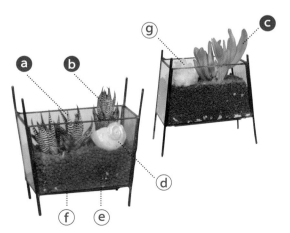

Plants

a Haworthiopsis attenuata (succulent, also known as zebra haworthia)

b Haworthia reinwardtii f. kaffirdriftensis (succulent)

c Crassula portulacea "Gollum" (succulent)

Materials

ⓓ Sea shell
ⓔ HydroBalls (fine clay pellets)
ⓕ Gravel (fine, white)
ⓖ Natural stone (quartz)

Containers

4¾" (12 cm) W at the widest point, 2" (5.5 cm) D, 4¾" (12 cm) H

Instructions

1. Put the gravel in the bottom.

2. Position the succulents and gently pour in the HydroBalls.

3. Arrange the sea shell and quartz.

An Adorable Terrarium with Animal Figures

Motoko Suzuki | Tokyo Fantastic Omotesando

This terrarium is designed to look like a miniature landscape in the savannah, shaded by a tree. Nelsol, a clay-like succulent growing medium that can be kneaded and molded into any shape, is used to depict an oasis in the savannah. Miniature animal figures, the stars of this scene, look like they are gathering around a watering hole.

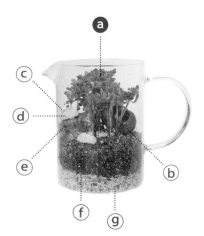

Plant
- **a** Aeonium sedifolium

Materials
- **b** Eucalyptus trumpet (dried plant)
- **c** Miniature figures
- **d** Gravel (medium, white)
- **e** Preserved moss (dried)
- **f** Nelsol (kneadable succulent growing medium). If you can't find Nelsol, use small clay pellets instead.
- **g** Zeolite

Containers
Outer diameter: 6" (15 cm)
Height: 5" (13 cm)

Instructions
1. Knead the Nelsol with water.
2. Pour the zeolite into the container and line with a flat layer of Nelsol balls.
3. Position the Aeonium sedifolium.
4. Roll more Nelsol into small balls and add to the container. Arrange the eucalyptus.
5. Put in the preserved moss. Glue the miniature figures to the stones and position them in the container.

Cacti Set in Vertical Flower Vases

Motoko Suzuki | Tokyo Fantastic Omotesando

Three terrariums created in long, narrow flower vases each contain a cactus-like Myrtillocactus geometrizans, a thin, white Euphorbia mammillaris "Variegata," and a cute Opuntia microdasys (bunny ears cactus) respectively. Lined up on a window sill or a shelf, the uniqueness of each cactus is hightlighted, creating a really fun display.

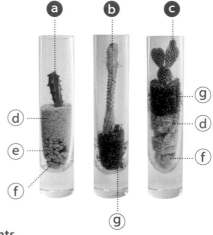

Plants
a Myrtillocactus geometrizans (cactus)
b Euphorbia mammillaris "Variegata" (cactus)
c Opuntia microdasys (bunny ears cactus)

Materials
d Zeolite
e Fine gravel (mix)
f Gravel (medium, gray)
g Nelsol (kneadable succulent growing medium) If you can't find Nelsol, use small clay pellets instead.

Containers
Outer diameter: 1¾" (4.5 cm)
Height: 8" (20 cm)

Instructions
1. Knead the Nelsol with water, and wrap it around the roots of each plant.
2. Put the fine and medium gravel in the first container, position the Myrtillocactus geometrizans, and pour zeolite around it using a funnel.
3. Fill the second container in the same way with the gravel, position the Euphorbia mammillaris, and pour zeolite around it using a funnel.
4. Fill the second container in the same way with the gravel, position the bunny ears cactus, and fill in around the plant with Nelsol balls.

A Striking Contemporary Design with a Venus Slipper Orchid

Motoko Suzuki | Tokyo Fantastic Omotesando

The Paphiopedilum or Venus slipper orchid is popular for its strange flower that looks like a carnivorous plant. Here it's planted in a large glass case with polka dots that match the black dots on the flower petals. Place this dramatic terrarium, which highlights the exotic flower within, in a room where people gather, like a living room, for a contemporary look.

Plant
ⓐ Paphiopedilum (Venus slipper orchid)

Materials
ⓑ HydroBalls (small)
ⓒ HydroBalls (large)
ⓓ Gravel (fine, white)

Container
9⅞" (25 cm) W x 4¾" (12 cm) D x 18" (46 cm) H

Instructions
1. Pour the gravel into the bottom of the container.
2. Place the orchid in the container, pot and all.
3. Add the large HydroBalls, followed by the small Hydroballs, until the pot is hidden.

Creation/Care Tips
Keep the orchid in its pot so that it can be taken out and repotted easily. Coordinate the dots on the petals with the dots on the container.

Cacti, Driftwood, Bark and Pumice Stones

Kazuto Kihara | Green Bucker

Choose a container with some height to display a tall, slim cactus. By combining the tall cactus with round, short cacti, as well as adding planting materials up to about half the height of the container, the finished display will be well balanced.

Plants
ⓐ Cleistocactus tarijensis (cactus)
ⓑ Cleistocactus tarijensis "Komachi" (cactus)

Materials
ⓒ Driftwood
ⓓ Coconut fiber rolled into a ball
ⓔ Bark chips
ⓕ Cactus growing medium (pumice, perlite, vermiculite, woody compost, etc.)
ⓖ Pumice stones (each about ⅓ to ½ inch (1 to 1.5 cm))

Container
4" (10 cm) W x 3" (8 cm) D x 8¼" (21 cm) H

Instructions
1. Line the bottom of the container with the pumice stones.
2. Position the cacti and the driftwood. Add the cactus-growing medium of your choice.
3. Put bark chips around the plants.
4. Put in the coconut fiber ball.

Creation/Care Tips
When handling the cacti, use chopsticks or tweezers so you don't stick yourself with the spines. Position the plant while keeping an eye on how they are balanced with each other. Fill the container about halfway full with the base material (the stones and the growing medium) for a well-balanced look.

Dried Materials with Air Plants in Jars

Kazuto Kihara | Green Bucker

Except for the air plants, all three of these jar terrariums have the same materials. Even with the same materials, by just changing the plant you can create very different looks. Display the Tillandsia caput-medusae terrarium with the lid open, which draws the eye to its unique shape.

Plants
- **(a)** Tillandsia ionantha (air plant)
- **(b)** Tillandsia caput-medusae (air plant)
- **(c)** Tillandsia brachycaulos (air plant)

Materials
- **(d)** Dried flowers of your choice (such as mini silver daisies)
- **(e)** Preserved moss (white, dried)
- **(f)** Tree nuts of your choice (such as tamarack cones)
- **(g)** Wood chips
- **(h)** Coconut fiber (brown)

Containers (3)
Outer diameter: 3½" (9 cm)
Height: 5½" (14 cm)

Instructions
1. Put the wood chips in the bottom of each container.
2. Lightly gather the coconut fiber into balls with your hands, and put one into each jar.
3. Add the tree nuts, dried flowers and preserved moss.
4. Position the air plants in each jar.

Air Plants Accented with a Splash of Blue

Kazuto Kihara | Green Bucker

This is an abundant terrarium packed with several dried plant materials and a Tillandsia brachycaulos air plant. When using lots of materials in a terrarium, make sure they aren't all the same height. Arrange them so the back of the terrarium is higher than the front for a stylish finish.

Plant
ⓐ Tillandsia brachycaulos (air plant)

Materials
ⓑ Preserved moss (dried)
ⓒ Dried flowers (delphinium, mini silver daisies, hydrangea)
ⓓ Tree nuts of your choice
ⓔ Coconut fiber
ⓕ Wood chips

Container
Outer diameter: 3½" (9 cm)
Height: 5½" (14 cm)

Instructions
1. Put the wood chips in the jar.
2. Lightly gather the coconut fiber into balls with your hands, and put one into each jar.
3. Add the tree nuts, dried flowers and preserved moss, keeping an eye on how well balanced the items are.
4. Position the Tillandsia brachycaulos.

Terrariums with a Southwestern Flair

Kazuto Kihara | Green Bucker

Even an empty food jar can become a stylish terrarium container when you wrap it with hemp twine. This is a lively terrarium that looks as if the cactus has grown right out of it. Since the container is so simple, choose a larger cactus to create impact.

Plants
a Gymnocalycium denudatum (cactus)
b Astrophytum myriostigma (cactus)

Materials
c Hemp twine
d Cactus growing medium (ground pumic, perlite, vermiculite, woody compost, etc.)

Containers (2)
Outer diameter: 1¾" (4.5 cm)
Height: 2½" (6.5 cm)

Instructions
1. Wrap the twine several times around the mouth of the jars.
2. Fill the jars about half full with the cactus-growing medium of your choice.
3. Position the cacti in each jar, and fill any gaps with more cactus-growing medium.

Glass Cup with Air Plants and Dried Fruit

Kazuto Kihara | Green Bucker

Make a simple terrarium using a cup you already have in your home. Here we've chosen some colorful dried fruit slices to complement the light green color of the Tillandsia paleacea major. Hang the terrarium with a hemp twine macramé hanger, or just display it on a table.

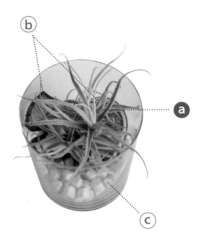

Plant
ⓐ Tillandsia paleacea major (air plant)

Materials
ⓑ Dried fruit slices
ⓒ Cedar wood balls

Container
Outer diameter: 3" (8 cm)
Height: 3½" (9 cm)

Instructions
1. Fill the bottom of the cup with cedar wood balls
2. Add the dried fruit slices.
3. Position the Tillandsia paleacea major.

A Collection of Cacti in their Natural Habitats

Kazuto Kihara | Green Bucker

For these simple cacti in beakers, we have used HydroBalls, which are round clay balls, as the growing medium. HydroBalls look cleaner and prettier than other mediums, and are perfect for use in glass containers. Coffee bean shaped garden picks are great accessories here.

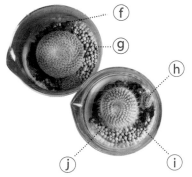

Materials
- (f) Coffee bean garden picks
- (g) Leather garden picks
- (h) Coconut fiber formed into balls
- (i) Wood chips
- (j) HydroBalls

Plants
- (a) Mammillaria herrerae (cactus)
- (b) Eriocactus leninghausii "golden ball" (cactus)
- (c) Gymnocalycium denudatum (cactus)
- (d) Orostachys Kinsei (cactus)
- (e) Echinocactus parryi (cactus)

Containers
Small
Outer diameter: 2⅔" (6.7 cm)
Height: 3½" (9 cm)
Medium
Outer diameter: 3" (7.8 cm)
Height: 4" (10.5 cm)
Large
Outer diameter: 3⅔" (9.2 cm)
Height: 4⅗" (12.1 cm)

Extra-large
Outer diameter: 4" (10 cm)
Height: 7⅔" (19.5 cm)

Instructions
1. Fill the beakers about ⅓ full with the HydroBalls.
2. Position the cacti, and add more HydroBalls around them.
3. Add some wood chips.
4. Decorate with coconut fiber balls, coffee bean picks, leather picks and and so on to your taste.

Creation/Care Tips
As with other growing mediums, HydroBalls should dry out thoroughly before watering them until they are evenly moist. Overwatering may lead to root rot, so be careful.

A Mystical Vision with Cacti, Volcanic Stone and Quartz

Kazuto Kihara | Green Bucker

This magical terrarium is centered by a volcanic rock surrounded by 5 different types and shapes of cacti plus a piece of quartz. Since each item is distinctive, use cacti that are all quite short for a uniform look. This should become a decorative centerpiece in your home.

Plants
ⓐ Echinofossulocactus zacatecasensis (cactus)
ⓑ Mammillaria spinosissima (cactus)
ⓒ Astrophytum ornatum (monk's hood cactus)
ⓓ Brasilicactus haselbergii (cactus)
ⓔ Gymnocalycium denudatum (cactus)

Materials
ⓕ Driftwood
ⓖ Natural stone (quartz)
ⓗ Volcanic stone
ⓘ Cactus-growing medium (pumice , perlite, vermiculite, woody compost, etc.)
ⓙ Pumice stones (each about ⅓ to ½ inch (1 to 1.5 cm)

Container
Outer diameter: 6" (15 cm)
Height: 9" (23 cm)

Instructions
1. Line the bottom of the container with the pumice stones.
2. Decide on the positions of the cacti and the driftwood. Add the cactus-growing medium to the container and position the cacti and driftwood.
3. Add some more pumice in the gaps.
4. Position the volcanic stone and the quartz.

Succulents, Dried Plants, Shredded Wood and Coconut Fibers

Kazuto Kihara | Green Bucker

The tallest beaker of the trio contains a twisty Tillandsia caput-medusae. Even though the three beakers are different sizes, they all contain the same level of shredded wood packing material and coconut fiber, with the air plants providing the variation in height. This creates a balanced look.

Plants
a Tillandsia caput-medusae (succulent)
b Tillandsia ionantha (succulent)
c Tillandsia brachycaulos (succulent)

Materials
d Curly moss (dried, white)
e Dried flowers of your choice (such as star corn, pepperberry, mini silver daisies, baby's breath, soft rice flowers etc.)
f Preserved moss (dried)
g Tree nuts of your choice (such as tamarack cones)
h Coconut fiber (white)
i Wood packing material

Containers
Small
Outer diameter: 3⅔" (9.2 cm)
Height: 4⅗" (12.1 cm)
Medium
Outer diameter: 3" (7.7 cm)
Height: 6" (15 cm)
Large
Outer diameter: 4" (10 cm)
Height: 7⅔" (19.5 cm)

Instructions
1. Put wood packing material in the bottom of each beaker.
2. Form the coconut fiber into soft balls and add to the beakers.
3. Put in dried flowers, tree nuts, curly moss and preserved moss.
4. Position the air plants in the order listed in the large, medium and small beakers.

Cacti and Driftwood in an Open Cylinder

Kazuto Kihara | Green Bucker

A fun terrarium that looks like the cacti are comparing each other's heights. By putting the smallest ones in the foreground and the taller ones in the mid-ground and back, you can give the landscape depth. The key is to put the volcanic rock in the background and the amethyst in a prominent location.

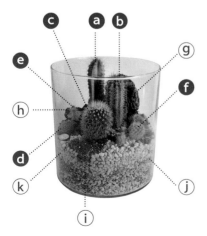

Plants
a Neocardenasia herzogiana (cactus)
b Weberbauerocereus johnsonii (cactus)
c Echeveria "Sirayukinohana" (cactus)
d Pachycereus pringlei (cactus)
e Eriocactus leninghausii (cactus)
f Mammillaria hahniana (cactus)

Materials
g Driftwood
h Volcanic rock
i Natural stone (amethyst)

j Cactus-growing medium (pumice, perlite, vermiculite, woody compost, etc.)
k Pumice stones

Container
Outer diameter: 7" (18 cm)
Height: 7½" (19 cm)

Instructions
1. Put the pumice stones in the bottom of the container.
2. Position the cacti and the driftwood, and add the cactus growing medium.
3. Add more pumice stones and the volcanic rock.
4. Put the amethyst in the foreground.

Air Plants with Driftwood and Denim

Kazuto Kihara | Green Bucker

One of the great things about terrariums that you can use any materials you like to decorate them. Here we have created a playful design by using denim scraps and leather picks in combination with the plants. Try placing this terrarium in an entranceway to greet guests as they enter your home.

Plants
a Tillandsia caput-medusae (air plant)
b Tillandsia ionantha (air plant)

Materials
c Driftwood
d Leather garden pick
e Denim scrap, tied into a ball with thin wire
f Sea shell
g White sand

Container
Outer diameter: 3½" (9 cm)
Height: 5½" (14 cm)

Instructions
1. Put the white sand in the bottom of the container.
2. Position the driftwood, sea shell, denim ball and leather picks in a well balanced manner.
3. Position the air plants.

Dried Flowers and Air Plants in a Curved Glass Jar

Kazuto Kihara | Green Bucker

This beautifully curved glass jar is filled with an especially luxuriantly decorated arrangement. Dried flowers are used in abundance to emphasize the undulating movements of the driftwood and Tillandsia caput-medusae. This refined terrarium is perfect for decorating a space where guests mingle.

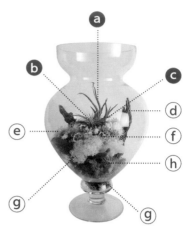

Plants
ⓐ Tillandsia caput-medusae (air plant)
ⓑ Tillandsia ionantha (air plant)
ⓒ Tillandsia brachycaulos (air plant)

Materials
ⓓ Driftwood branch
ⓔ Dried flowers (mini silver daisies, everlasting, winged everlasting, etc.)
ⓕ Curly moss (dried)
ⓖ Preserved moss (dried, white and brown)
ⓗ Coconut fiber (brown)

Container
Outer diameter: 8¼" (21 cm)
Height: 21⅔" (55 cm)

Instructions
1. Put the preserved moss in the bottom of the container.
2. Position the driftwood branch.
3. Add coconut fiber, dried flowers and curly moss over the driftwood branch.
4. Position the air plants in the center.

Creation/Care Tips
When decorating a large container like this, make sure that the design doesn't become lopsided. Aim for positioning shorter elements in the front and taller ones in the middle and back.

Air Plants, Moss and Pine Cones in Autumn Colors

Kazuto Kihara | Green Bucker

Air plants such as Tillandsia ionantha and Tillandsia brachycaulos, with their beautiful leaves, are all-around all stars who play well with any kind of materials. Try arranging them with materials such as pine cones and tree nuts for an autumn-themed combination. Brown tree nuts go well with red-hued dried flowers.

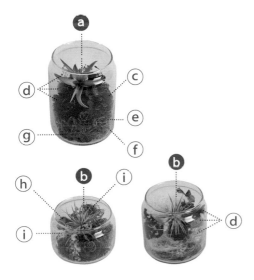

Plants
ⓐ Tillandsia ionantha (air plant)
ⓑ Tillandsia brachycaulos (air plant)

Materials
ⓒ Dried cones, nuts and seed pods of your choice (pine cones, dried mallow seed pods, tamarack cones, etc.)
ⓓ Dried flowers of your choice (hydrangeas, everlasting, baby's breath, globe thistle, etc.)
ⓔ Curly moss (dried, green)
ⓕ Coconut fiber (brown)
ⓖ Bark chips
ⓗ Twigs cut into short pieces
ⓘ Curly moss (dried, white and brown)

Container
Small
Outer diameter: 3½" (9 cm)
Height: 4⅓" (11 cm)
Medium
Outer diameter: 3½" (9 cm)
Height: 5½" (14 cm)
Large
Outer diameter: 3½" (9 cm)
Height: 6⅔" (17 cm)

Instructions
1. Put the bark chips in the bottom of the container.
2. Lightly form the coconut fiber into a ball and put into the container.
3. Arrange the tree nuts, dried flowers, curly moss and twigs in the container, with an eye towards balance.
4. Position the air plants.

Beakers with Air Plants and Dried Flowers in Muted Colors

Kazuto Kihara | Green Bucker

A beaker that may remind you of a school science lab becomes a cute decorative piece when it's used in a terrarium. Use pale materials and light-colored plants for a soft, gentle look, with splashes of color provided by dried flowers.

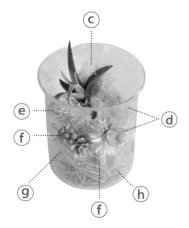

Plants
ⓐ Tillandsia brachycaulos (air plant)
ⓑ Tillandsia ionantha (air plant)

Materials
ⓒ Preserved moss (dried, white)
ⓓ Dried flowers of your choice (such as hydrangeas, everlasting rice flowers, mini silver daisies etc.)
ⓔ Curly moss (dried, white)
ⓕ Dried tree nuts, cones, seed pods of your choice (such as tamarack cones)
ⓖ Coconut fiber (white)
ⓗ Wood packing material

Instructions
1. Put the wood packing materials in the bottom of the container.
2. From the coconut fiber into a ball and put into the container.
3. Add the preserved moss, dried flowers, curly moss and tree nuts and cones.
4. Position the air plants.

Collect Seasonal Materials for Your Terrariums

① Tree nuts (tamarack cones, metasequoia cones)
② Dried flowers (Ammobium or winged everlasting)
③ Sea shells
④ Dried flowers (French phylica)
⑤ Preserved moss
⑥ Preserved flowers (minature silver daisies)
⑦ Cypress wood chips

Terrarium materials are not limited to plants, stones and branches. If you look around, you can find that there is an abundance of materials you can use. By varying the items you add to a terrarium according to the season, you can enjoy them throughout the year even more.

For example, in the fall you can collect pine cones and acorns that have fallen to the ground. In the summer you can gather sea shells, and in the winter try using wintry looking dried flowers and plants, which you can make yourself by hanging plants upside down or drying them in silica gel. Brightly colored preserved flowers can easily add a springtime mood to your terrariums and go well with light colored wood chips.

By using materials you have collected yourself in your terrariums, they can evoke happy memories whenever you see them.

Succulent Leaves Rising from a Bed of Sand

Yuya Ohyama | Pianta×Stanza

A well-grown Curio repens (Senecio repens) succulent with vertical leaves is planted in a container that's just big enough for it, for a lively look. The breezy, light design is enhanced by the pale decorative stones on the sand. There are several varieties of Curio repens with interestingly shaped leaves, which makes them well suited for planting on their own.

Plant
ⓐ Curio repens or Senecio repens (succulent)

Materials
ⓑ Pebbles (medium, white)
ⓒ Sand (white)

Container
Outer diameter: 3¾" (6.5 cm)
Height: 5½" (14 cm)

Instructions
1. Pour about 1⅓ inches (3 cm) of sand into the container.
2. Position the succulent, and pour more sand around it.
3. Surround the succulent with pebbles.

Moss, Ferns and Ficus in a Large Jar

Yuya Ohyama | Pianta×Stanza

The airy light leaves of a Davallia tyermannii fern fill a fairly large glass container. The pale roots of the fern and the green, leathery leaves of the ficus accent this terrarium. The moss adds a forest-like feel.

Plants
ⓐ Davallia tyermannii (fern)
ⓑ Ficus microcarpa (indoor plant)
ⓒ Leucobryum juniperoideum (moss)

Materials
ⓓ A mixture of red clay pellets and plant growing soil/medium
ⓔ Gravel (fine, black)

Container
Outer diameter: 5½" (14 cm)
Height: 7⅞" (20 cm)

Instructions
1. Put a ⅓ inch (1 cm) layer of gravel in the bottom of the container.
2. Put in about 1⅓ inches (3 cm) of combined clay pellets and growing medium.
3. Position the fern and the ficus.
4. Lay the moss around the foot of the fern.
5. Add more growing medium up to the level of the roots of the moss.

Creation/Care Tips
Arrange the moss so that it looks as if it's pouring over the ground.

Ferns, Succulents and Moss in an Open Container

Yuya Ohyama | Pianta×Stanza

The feathery, breezy leaves of the asparagus fern and the cute round leaves of the million hearts plants are the main features of this terrarium. The moss is used to create a natural-looking landscape, using large and small leaved parts. This is a very comforting terrarium to gaze at. You can also switch out the miniature figures as the plants grow.

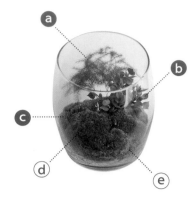

Plants
ⓐ Asparagus plumosus var. nanus (fern)
ⓑ Dischidia ruscifolia (succulent, common name million hearts)
ⓒ Leucobryum juniperoideum (moss)

Materials
ⓓ Miniature figures
ⓔ Sphagnum (peat moss)

Container
Outer diameter: 4" (10 cm)
Height: 6" (15 cm)

Instructions
1. Moisten the sphagnum moss, and put about a ¾ to 1 inch (2 cm) layer in the bottom of the container.
2. Position the asparagus fern. Gently shake the soil clinging to the root off, wrap the roots in some moistened sphagnum moss, and plant.
3. Plant the succulent in the same way.
4. Spread out the moss on the ground.
5. Glue the miniature figures onto round wood chips cut in half using a glue gun. Bury the wood chips with the figures in the moss to fix them in place.

Creation/Care Tips
Instead of just laying the moss evenly, try selecting bits that have different heights to give a flow to the design and make it look like a mountain landscape inside.

Delightful Succulents in Stackable Jars

Yuya Ohyama | Pianta×Stanza

Stacking containers used as terrariums are great when space is limited. You can also change the stacking order occasionally to enjoy them in a new light. Both echeverias and kalanchoes turn red in the fall, so they add some seasonal variety as well.

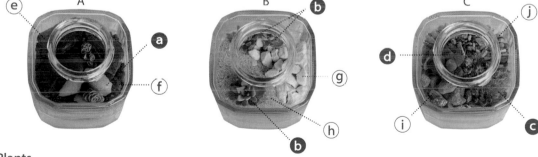

Plants
a Echeveria (succulent, variety unknown)
b Kalanchoe (succulent, variety unknown)
c Leucobryum juniperoideum (moss)
d Haworthia obtusa (succulent)

Materials
e Pebbles (medium, black)
f Gravel (fine, black)
g Pebbles (small, white)
h Sand (white)
i Pebbles (small, gray)
j Gravel (fine, gray)

Containers (each)
3" (8 cm) W x 3" (8 cm) D x 2¾" (7 cm) H

Instructions
1. Fill the bottom of the containers with gravel or sand.
2. Position the succulents and add gravel or sand around them.
3. Layer the moss into the C container only.
4. Add pebbles around the succulents.

Covered Jars with Cryptanthus and Gravel

Yuya Ohyama | Pianta×Stanza

Star-shaped Cryptanthus plants planted singly in glass jars make for very pretty accents in your space. Cryptanthus comes in many colors and patterns, including ones with spots or stripes. Try coordinating them with decorative colored sand in the container and line up several jars.

Plant
ⓐ Cryptanthus (indoor plant)

Materials
ⓑ Gravel (fine, black)
ⓒ Gravel (fine, gray)

Container
Outer diameter: 2½" (6.5 cm)
Height: 5½" (14 cm)

Instructions
1. Put about ⅓ inch (1 cm) of gravel in the container.
2. Position the Cryptanthus and push the roots into the gravel slightly using tweezers. Add another ⅓ inch (1 cm) of gravel to finish.

Creation/Care Tips
If the leaves of the Cryptanthus spread out too much they may get damaged by the sides of the container. It's a good idea to cut off the larger lower leaves before putting the plant in the container.

Mini Terrariums with Succulents in a Gravel Bed

Yuya Ohyama | Pianta×Stanza

Two small terrariums in different sizes that fit in the palm of your hand. The key is to level out each layer of material added, so that the terrariums look neat even from the side. Both Crassulas and Sempervivums like sunlight and will flower if the conditions are right, so put them on a bright window sill and turn them occasionally as you enjoy watching them grow.

Plants
ⓐ Crassula (succulent, variety unknown)
ⓑ Sempervivum (succulent, variety unknown)

Material
ⓒ Stones (medium, white)
ⓓ Gravel (fine, white)
ⓔ Sand (white)
ⓕ Stones (medium, gray)
ⓖ Gravel (fine, black)
ⓗ Succulent growing medium

Containers
Large 2¾" (7 cm) square
Small 2⅓" (6 cm) square

Instructions
1. Put about ⅓ inch (1 cm) each of sand and stones to each container.
2. Add some growing medium to the small container only.
3. Add gravel to both containers, and position the succulents.
4. Add some stones around the sides of the containers a few at a time.

Succulents in a Sealed Jar

Yuya Ohyama | Pianta×Stanza

Three succulents with different leaf shapes are planted together in this terrarium. There are so many different shapes and colors of succulents you can have fun choosing the ones that speak to you. Plant them together quite closely so that the design always looks interesting.

Plants
a Crassula muscosa (succulent)
b Crassula (succulent, variety unknown)
c Dischidia ruscifolia (succulent, common name Million hearts)

Materials
d Pumice stones (small)
e Clay pellets (small)

Container
Outer diameter: 2½" (6.5 cm)
Height: 5½" (14 cm)

Instructions
1. Put some clay pellets in the bottom of the container.
2. Position the succulents, and add more clay pellets around them.
3. Add the pumice stones.

Stories in Miniature in a Terrarium Village

Yuya Ohyama | Pianta×Stanza

In these terrariums, the moss is used as backdrops to the miniature figures, depicting tiny landscapes. You can create all kinds of stories by just adding branches and stones into the glass containers. Line up several containers with different shapes, and create your very own fantasy world.

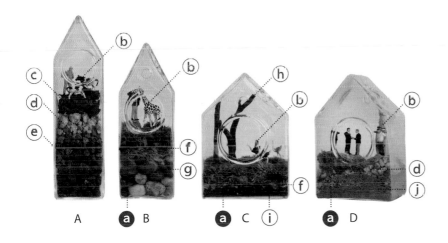

Plant
ⓐ Leucobryum juniperoideum (moss)

Containers
A 2¾" (7 cm) square
B 2⅓" (6 cm) square
C and **D** 2⅓" (6 cm) square

Material
ⓑ Miniature figures
ⓒ Bark chips
ⓓ Gravel (mix)
ⓔ Clay pellets (medium)
ⓕ Sphagnum moss
ⓖ Pebbles (medium, mix)
ⓗ Tree branch
ⓘ Gravel (fine, black)
ⓙ Sand

Instructions

Containers B, C and D
1. Add the sand, gravel and pebbles in the containers in layers.
2. Put moistened sphagnum moss into containers B and C only.
3. Lay in the Leucobryum juniperoideum moss.
4. Glue the miniature figures onto pebbles or tree branches.
5. When you want to stand up a minature figure in the moss, fix the feet with wire.
6. Fix the Leucobryum juniperoideum moss in place with wire.

Container A
1. Put clay pellets, gravel and bark chips in the container.
2. Glue the miniature figures onto pieces of bark chip, and fix in place.

Fantasy Landscapes Contained in Round Corked Jars

Yuya Ohyama | Pianta×Stanza

Fantasy landscapes are created in miniature in these round corked jars using succulents and miniature cow figures. Try making scenes that look as if they are under water using succulents too. Take advantage of the shape of the container by leaving plenty of space in the center and planting up the edges on the left and right, to create a mini tableau.

Plants
ⓐ Aeonium arboreum (succulent, variety unknown)
ⓑ Crassula muscosa (succulent)
ⓒ Senecio (succulent, variety unknown)
ⓓ Dischidia ruscifolia (succulent)
ⓔ Leucobryum juniperoideum (moss)

Materials
ⓕ Pebbles (medium, mix)
ⓖ Gravel (fine, gray)
ⓗ Sand (black)
ⓘ Miniature figures
ⓙ Gravel (medium, white)
ⓚ Sand (white)

Containers (2)
Outer diameter: 2¾" (7 cm)
Height: 2¾" (7 cm)

Instructions
Container A
1. Put sand in the bottom of the container.
2. Add gravel and plant the **ⓐ** and **ⓑ** succulents.
3. Add pebbles in the spaces around the plants.

Container B
1. Put sand in the bottom of the container.
2. Add gravel and plant the **ⓒ** and **ⓓ** succulents.
3. Layer the "ground" with moistened Leucobryum juniperoideum (moss).
4. Affix the miniature figures into the moss with wire (see page 69).

Rustic Air Plants and Driftwood in Covered Jars

Yuya Ohyama | Pianta×Stanza

Air plants are positioned on top of layers of pebbles and gravel along with driftwood to create desert and seashore scenes. Add clay pellets and growing medium or soil for an even more natural look. Position air plants above and below the branches of the tall driftwood in a trapezoidal shape for a balanced look.

Plants
a Tillandsia ionantha (air plant)
b Tillandsia capitata (air plant)
c Tillandsia bulbosa

Materials
(d) Driftwood
(e) Pebbles (small, gray)
(f) Gravel (medium, black)
(g) Red clay pellets (small)
(h) Succulent growing medium
(i) Gravel (fine, black)

Containers (2)
Outer diameter: 5½" (8.5 cm)
Height: 7½" (19 cm)

Instructions
Container A
1. Put about 2 inches (5 cm) of pebbles in the bottom of the container.
2. Fix the driftwood in place by burying it a bit in the pebbles.
3. Hang the air plants under the driftwood or between its branches.

Containers B
1. Put about ⅓ inch (1 cm) of gravel in the bottom of the container.
2. Add layers of pebbles, then growing medium. Each layer should be about ¾ inch (2 cm) deep.
3. Add about ⅓ inch (1 cm) of clay pellets, then some more gravel.
4. Fix the driftwood in place by burying it a bit.
5. Position the air plants under the driftwood.

A Moss Ball with Succulents in a Glass Globe

Yuya Ohyama | Pianta×Stanza

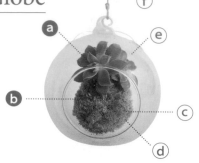

A kokedama, or moss ball, combined with a round container creates a very pretty terrarium which looks good from any angle. Position an Aeonium as though it's a flower growing out of the kokedama to make it even more adorable. Try hanging from a kitchen counter or the ceiling—hanging terrariums like this are really easy to display.

Plants
a Aeonium arboreum (succulent, variety unknown)
b Leucobryum juniperoideum (moss)

Materials
ⓒ Sphagnum moss
ⓓ Thread
ⓔ Fishing line
ⓕ Hemp twine

Container
Outer diameter: 4" (10 cm)

Instructions
1. Shake the soil off the roots of the Aeonium arboreum and wrap them in some moistened sphagnum moss.
2. Press the sphagnum moss a little to form a ball and wrap with thread (or thin wire) several times.
3. Wrap the sphagnum moss ball with Leucobryum juniperoideum moss. Wind with string to form a kokedama (moss ball).
4. Thread fishing line through the middle of the kokedama vertically. Pass the fishing wire through the 2 holes in the container to fix in place.
5. Pass twine through the top of the container and hang at the height you desire.

A Family of Ducks in a Whimsical Setting

Yuya Ohyama | Pianta×Stanza

A verdant waterside scene is created with Crassula and miniature duck figures. A small forest is depicted in the background using Leucobryum juniperoideum moss and dried Spanish moss. Add a miniature figure and a fence to the scene to make it even more lively. A Crassula that blooms in the spring with small pink flowers, such as Crassula rupestris, is recommended.

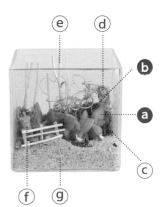

Plants
a Crassula (succulent, variety unknown)
b Leucobryum juniperoideum (moss)

Materials
c Sphagnum moss
d Dried Spanish moss
e Twigs
f Miniature figures
g Sand (white)

Container
2⅓" (6 cm) wide x 2⅓" (6 cm) deep x 2" (5 cm) high

Instructions
1. Put sand in the bottom of the container.
2. Position the Crassula.
3. Add some more sand to firmly fix the plant into place.
4. Layer the ground with moistened Leucobryum juniperoideum moss.
5. Position the sphagnum moss, twigs and Spanish moss in that order. Push the sphagnum moss firmly in place by poking it with tweezers. Bury the twigs securely in the gravel too.
6. Fix the figures in place by wrapping fine wire around the feet and sticking the wire into the sand (see page 69). Glue the ducks onto a wooden base, then place on the sand.

Plant Glossary

Here are some of the plants used in this book as well as other ones that we recommend for terrariums.

Tillandsias (Air Plants)

Tillandsia tectorum

This air plant has thin leaves that grow in a spiral, which make them look like pom poms. The silvery white hair that grows on the leaves are called trichomes and help the plant to draw in moisture from the air. There are varieties that grow to about 6 inches in diameter, and ones that grow up to 2 feet (61 cm). Water them 2 to 3 times a week by misting them in the spring and summer, and about once a week in the fall and winter.

Tillandsia caput-medusae

"Caput-medusae" comes from the Greek mythological creature Medusa, who has writhing snakes as hair. These twisting, contorted leaves that rise from the vase-shaped bottom are thought to resemble Medusa's hair. Because it's a silver-leaf type of tillandsia, the leaves are covered with trichomes. Water them two to three times a week by misting them very well, then make sure to dry out the roots thoroughly before returning them to the container.

Tillandsia ionantha

This is one of the major silver-leaved tillandsias; "ionantha" means "violet colored" in Latin. When it flowers a long, thin shoot emerges from the crown and bears bright purple blossoms. At the same time the leaves turn bright red and yellow really putting on a show. There are many varieties that comes in a range of sizes. Water them once or twice a week by misting them thoroughly.

Tillandsia funckiana

Another well known type of the silver leaf tillandsias. The thin, needle-like leaves grow from the base and up the stems. Small suckers or plants form between the leaves and stems. Although it looks like an evergreen tree branch, the leaves are quite soft to the touch. Once a plant has grown to about 4 inches (10 cm) in height, large bright red flowers may bloom. Water them two to three times a week by misting them very well. They are very susceptible to winter cold, so be sure to keep the temperature of their environment above 50 degrees F (10 degrees C).

Tillandsia ionantha Fuego

This is a type of Tillandsia ionantha that changes into a bright color as it grows. "Fuego," which means "fire" or "blaze" in Spanish, is also the name of a volcano in Guatemala; the plant is called this because the leaves turn a bright red when the plant flowers. The photo shows a clump of these plants. The more plants there are in a clump, the more showy the flowers and leaves. Water them once or twice a week by misting them thoroughly.

Tillandsia useneoides (Spanish moss)

One of the best known tillandsias, with curly, hair-like hangling silver leaves. In its native habitat it grows by hanging from trees, so in order to grow this you should hang it from something most of the time. Once it has grown about 12 to 16 inches (30 to 50 cm) long, it may have tiny flowers. Water them two to three times a week by misting them very well, then dry them by hanging them up in an airy place.

Tillandsia heteromorpha
A rare type of silver leaf tillandsia. Although it is similar to Tillandsia funckiana, this has longer leaves that open up to the outside. If it grows well, the stem becomes elongated, and side shoots or suckers form between the leaves and the stem. The flowering period is very short, but the pink bracts and the purple flowers form a beautiful color gradation. Water them once or twice a week by misting them thoroughly.

Tillandsia paraceamajor
This is a rather unusual silver leaf tillandsia. Thick, twisty leaves with lots of movement grow out of an elongated stem. The leaves are covered with a lot of trichomes, so that they look very pale. If it grows well and the stem becomes longer, a lot of suckers or sideshoots form. You can also grow the plants in large clumps. Water them once or twice a week by misting them thoroughly.

Mosses

Racomitrium japonicum (sunagoke moss)
Sunagoke moss (which means "sand moss") looks like a group of tiny stars massed together. It is a moss that is very resistant to drought and dry conditions relatively speaking. Because it grows even in full sunlight, it is a widely seen moss in Japan. Although it grows upwards, the stems stop at around 1⅓ to 2 inches (1–5 cm) in height and stop growing. This sturdy moss only needs to be watered about once every two weeks, or whenever the surface looks dry.

Pogonatum cirratum
Grows wild in western regions of Japan. In Japanese this moss is called "Hohrai pine moss," because its upright stems with their thin, needle-like leaves look like pine trees. (Hohrai is the name of a sacred mountain in China which appears in classic literature and art.) It propagates by sending out spores from thin sporytes that grow from the stems. Water it about once a week by misting it well with a spray bottle. It doesn't withstand drought and dryness well, so keep it in a sealed, humid environment and adjust the ambient temperature so that it doesn't get "cooked" inside the container.

Fissidens japonicus Doz. et Molk
Called "phoenix moss" in Japan; the name comes from the wing-like appearance of the stems and leaves which spread to the side as they grow. This moss mainly grows in mountainous areas or in between rocks along a stream. Since it grows in water as well as soil, it is also used as an aquarium plant and is sold at tropical fish shops. Water it well by misting it frequently so that the surface never dries out.

Conocephalum conicum (snakeskin liverwort)
This moss grows by spreading itself along the ground and has large, flat leaves. In Japanese it's called "snake moss" because the leaves look like the scales on a snake. The undersides of the leaves are covered with many thin, white roots which cling fast to whatever surface it is on. Water this moss about once every two weeks by misting it thoroughly with a spray bottle.

Rhodobryum giganteum (rose moss)
This moss is called "big umbrella moss" in Japan, because the large open leaves look like umbrellas. It is one of the bigger moss varieties, with fresh green leaves that shimmer when they are fully watered and is one of the most beautiful Japanese moss varieties. Since they have relatively long roots, they need to be planted with care so as not to damage the roots. Water them about once every two weeks by misting them thoroughly.

Leucobryum juniperoidum (smaller white moss)
This is a very popular moss in Japan and sold in most garden and home centers. Its common name in Japanese is "mountain moss," although that name is often used for two other types of mosses. It is a very drought-resistant moss relatively speaking, and is used for bonsai as well as kokedama (moss balls). Depending on what other mosses it is combine with, it's better to seal the container you plant it in. Water about once every two weeks by misting it thoroughly with a spray bottle.

Succulents are divided into types depending on the seasons in which they have growth spurts and thus, need to be watered more. For example, a spring-fall type needs watering once a week in the spring and fall while it's growing actively, once every two weeks in the summer, and once a month in the winter.

Callisia repens (creeping inchplant)
Spring-fall type
Native to Central and South America, this succulent is also called "training dew plant" in Japanese. The small, leaves are layered like rose petals and when as they grow they become red. Water sparingly, about once every two weeks, and keep on the dry side. It spreads in all directions as it grows, so if it outgrows its container you will need to replant it.

Crassula portulacea f. monstrosa (jade plant)
Spring-fall type
The cylindrical green leaves of this succulent have a shiny, smooth surface and the tips are red and indented. As the plant grows, the lower leaves fall off, exposing the bumpy trunk-like stem, so that it looks like a strange miniature alien tree, which is why a common name for it in Japanese is space tree. Water about once every two weeks in general, whenever the soil is dry. Water sparingly in the winter.

Echeveria secunda
Spring-fall type
The "secunda" part of this echiveria's name means that the stems and roots spread out flat. As that indicates, the stems of this unusual looking plant connect to each other in a ribbon-like pattern as it grows. The leaves turn red between the fall and spring and in the spring and summer small flowers may bloom. Water it once a week during its growing period and when it is dormant scale it down to about once every two weeks.

Lithops lesliei (stone plants)
Winter type
With pairs of large, swollen leaves stuck together, this lithops, or stone plant, has a cute look. It flowers in the fall and sheds its outer layer in winter to spring. If you overwater it while it's shedding, the new shoots may shed too, so watch out for that. You can divide the clumps when you repot. Water about every two weeks, when the soil is dry.

Haworthia obtusa
Spring-fall type
The plump, round leaves and the translucent tips that sparkle in light characterize this succulent. The Japanese name for it means dew stone. Avoid putting it in direct sunlight but choose a bright, well-lit location indoors for it. If there isn't enough light it may become leggy, as the stems grow long when the plant reaches for the light. Water about once a week, when the soil is dry. In the winter, check the plant and water even less.

Haworthia pilifera
Spring-fall type
Of the many varieties of haworthia piliferas, this one stands out for its leaves that are covered with tiny thin hairs. Since it forms clumps by growing chicks or offsets from its base, you can propagate it easily by dividing the clumps. You can also take leaf cuttings, which root easily. Water about once every two weeks, when the soil is dry, and hold back on watering even more in the winter.

Pachyphytum oviferum (moonstones)
Spring-fall type
This succulent's plump, round leaves look as if they have been dusted with a white powder. In Japanese it is called a "star beauty." As it grows upwards, sometimes the stems become unable to bear the weight of the leaves, so trim the stems near the base diligently to encourage the plant to grow low and sideways. In the fall, the leaves take on a pale pink color. Water about once every two weeks and keep it on the dry side.

Kalanchoe tomentosa (panda plant, pussy ears, chocolate soldiers)
Spring-fall type
The Japanese name for this kalanchoe is "moon rabbit ears" because the leaves are covered with fine, white hairs. The oval shaped leaves have spiky ends, which are colored chocolate brown. Although it's a succulent that likes bright light, even sunlight, it should be placed out of direct sun. Water about once every two weeks when the soil is dry, and try not to water it much at all in the winter.

Mammillaria martinezii

A cactus that is characterized by its rounded shape that is covered with white spikes. It produces chicks or offsets from the base and in the winter it may produce small pink flowers. It prefers a sunny location, so give it plenty of sunlight during the day such as on a windowsill, and water it sparingly, about once every two weeks.

Euphorbia horrida (African milk barrel)

Spring-summer type
Although its spikes make it look like a cactus, this is a succulent. The "horrida" part of its botanical name means that it has many spines, but the parts that look like spines are actually the flower bracts left over after the flowers have dropped off, that remain on the plant for a long time afterwards. During the spring to summer growing season, water it whenever the soil is dry. In the winter, water sparingly.

Huernia brevirostris

Called "mosquito horns" in Japanese, the thin, stick-like stems and branches of this cactus are covered with prickly spines. Although it is usually bright green in color, in the winter it changes to a reddish purple. In the summer, yellow star-shaped flowers blooms around the base of the plant. Put this in an airy location during the summer and water about three times a month.

Echinocereus pentalophus cv. momotarou (ladyfinger cactus)

This is a variety of Echinocereus pentalophus called Momotaro, or Peach Boy, a figure from Japanese folklore. It's a cactus hybrid with no spines, and small white areole without spines. In the spring it blooms with large pink flowers. Make sure the container it's in has good ventilation and place in an airy location during the summer. Water about three times a month.

Echinocereus rigidissimus (rainbow cactus)

Called "purple sun" in Japanese, this cactus is characterized by its oval shape that's a bit bigger at the top and its reddish-purple color. In early spring large, pink flowers bloom, and chicks or offsets form around the bottom. It does well in sunlight. Water about three times a month and in the winter water very sparingly, if at all.

Gymnocalycium horridispinum

The "horridispinum" part of its botanical name means "scary spines," and indeed this cactus has some long, sharp spines growing out randomly. In Japanese it's called a "dinosaur ball." In contrast to its intimidating appearance, its flowers are large and bright pink and many people consider it one of the most beautiful blooming cacti. Water it once ever two to three weeks, and water sparingly in the winter.

Other Plants (ferns)

Selaginella remotifolia

Although this is called kurama moss in Japan, this plant is actually an evergreen fern. It grows in clusters in the wild in shady, humid spots such as in the shade of rocks, rather like mosses. The long, twisting stems with small rice grain shaped leaves spread along the ground. As with mosses, water about once every two weeks by misting it well. Keep in a sealed container to maintain humidity.

Lycopodium Brassii Little John

A fern that is native to tropical forests and other humid locations, that is characterized by its twisting, drooping growing habit. It does well in humid growing conditions like the ones mosses prefer, so it works well in terrariums. Water every two to three weeks by misting it well. Water even less than that in the winter.

Comments from the Designers

"A world within glass.

How is it possible to recreate the landscape you envision in a small space? How do you use dried plants and materials, and how do you decorate with various objects? Terrariums are created by expanding the world that exists within your own unique imagination.

I feel that the current popularity of terrariums has grown along with the increasing interest in using slow growing, low-maintenance plants such as succulents, air plants and mosses in interiors. Whenever I make a new terrarium, I start by deciding on the container, and then the plants, in that order. Looking for the right container is so much fun, and once I have the right container, I can envision the finished landscape. Containers made for terrariums aren't the only ones you can use. Try using glass jars meant for kitchen use, any glass bottle you have on hand and so on, and arrange your plants in them. When a plant is enclosed in clear glass, you may find that it looks quite different. Create your own original terrariums using driftwood, decorative stones, dried flowers and so on and make sure the environment is suitable for the plants you've chosen. I hope you'll enjoy creating your own small worlds."

— Sueko Katsuji

Buriki no Zyoro
3-6-15 Jiyugaoka, Meguro-ku, Tokyo
Hours: 10:00–19:00 (open all year)
www.buriki.jp

"Terrariums are becoming very popular recently as a way of easily enjoying plants indoors. In our store, we are carrying more terrariums as well. Ready-made terrariums sold in stores are beautiful, but probably the best way to enjoy terrariums is to gather the materials you like, and arrange them yourself within a small glassed-in space.

The things you put into a terrarium will vary depending on what kinds of plants you choose for it. It's a good idea to collect a stash of nuts, seashells, fabric or leather scraps, rusty metal parts and nails and so on, and put them in a pretty container, to use as materials for your terrariums as well as a source of inspiration.

For this book, we have created several terrariums combining air plants and dried flowers. We think they are much more colorful than what you'd expect from terrariums. Air plants are easy to maintain too. We hope you'll try making your own terrariums using these plants."

— Kazuto Kihara

Green Bucker
www.greenbucker.com
Facebook: https://www.facebook.com/green.bucker/

"Tokyo Fantastic Omotesando is a flower boutique with the concept, 'Let's Enjoy Japan.' I (Tida Flower) have a lot of fun designing special, one-of-a-kind flower arrangements every day for the store. My central theme these days is to recreate the emotions we felt when we gathered wildflowers as children; that feeling of capturing the beauty and strength of flowers that grow in their native habitat, and bringing that life force indoors. So the designs I create exist in a natural world, one that intersects with natural forest land.

Terrariums, where you can create a small, concentrated version of natural landscapes, are highly recommended as objects to brighten your home. In our store, we also make 'flower bottles,' which are glass medicine containers filled with dried flowers.

I hope you will envision small worlds that bring joy to your heart every day as you make your own small original creations."

— Motoko Suzuki (Tida Flower)

Tokyo Fantastic Omotesando
3-16-6 Minami Aoyama, Minato-ku, Tokyo
Hours: 12:00–19:00 (closed Wednesdays)
blog.tokyofantastic.jp
Instagram: @tidatomoko

"Terrariums are a way to enjoy living plants in glass containers, but we hope that by including miniatures, you will be inspired to imagine a whole story going on within that small space. You can have so much fun arranging the little objects you've assembled, stacking them, hanging them and so on to decorate your little universe. In addition, you can also enjoy viewing it from various angles, and discovering the different landscapes that reveal themselves. That's the fun of a terrarium. Try looking at it from straight above, or from the side. There's a whole other dimension to enjoying terrariums that sets them apart from ordinary plants in pots.

Terrariums, perhaps more than any other interior arrangements, are the most suited to blending with your existing decor. But of course, they contain living plants. Don't forget that you need to take care of them. If you choose the right place for your terrarium that suits the environment the plants need, maintaining them shouldn't be too hard. I hope you'll create your own 'one of a kind' miniature gardens, that you can't resist peeking into. I couldn't be happier if the projects in this book will inspire you to use everyday glass containers to easily incorporate living plants into your life."

— Yuya Ohyama

Pianta×Stanza
Chuo Ward, Tokyo
Hours: 11:00–20:00 (closed Thursdays)
http://pianta-stanza.jp/
This book includes terrariums created by Pianta×Stanza staff members.

"Books to Span the East and West"

Tuttle Publishing was founded in 1832 in the small New England town of Rutland, Vermont (USA). Our core values remain as strong today as they were then—to publish best-in-class books which bring people together one page at a time. In 1948, we established a publishing office in Japan—and Tuttle is now a leader in publishing English-language books about the arts, languages and cultures of Asia. The world has become a much smaller place today and Asia's economic and cultural influence has grown. Yet the need for meaningful dialogue and information about this diverse region has never been greater. Over the past seven decades, Tuttle has published thousands of books on subjects ranging from martial arts and paper crafts to language learning and literature—and our talented authors, illustrators, designers and photographers have won many prestigious awards. We welcome you to explore the wealth of information available on Asia at **www.tuttlepublishing.com.**

Published by Tuttle Publishing, an imprint of Periplus Editions (HK) Ltd.

www.tuttlepublishing.com

Boutique Mook No. 1354 OSHARE NA SHOKUBUTSUEN TERRARIUM
Copyright © 2017 BOUTIQUE SHA
English translation rights arranged with BOUTIQUE-SHA, INC through Japan UNI Agency, Inc., Tokyo

Staff (Original Japanese Edition)
Editor in chief Ryohei Maruyama
Editing and production Dome Co.
Photography Yumiko Miyazawa, Miyuki Teraoka
Art direction Ren Ehara (mashroom design)
Design Yuki Maeda, Ayumi Horikawa (mashroom design)
Writing assistance Ayumi Goya, Yayoi Tatsu
Copy editing Gento Shorin Ltd.
Editor Yoshiaki Fukuda
Publisher Akira Naito
Published by Boutique-sha Co.

English Translation © 2021 by Periplus Editions (HK) Ltd.
Translated from Japanese by Makiko Itoh

ISBN 978-0-8048-5407-8

Distributed by
North America, Latin America & Europe
Tuttle Publishing
364 Innovation Drive, North Clarendon
VT 05759-9436 U.S.A.
Tel: 1 (802) 773-8930
Fax: 1 (802) 773-6993
info@tuttlepublishing.com
www.tuttlepublishing.com

Asia Pacific
Berkeley Books Pte. Ltd.
3 Kallang Sector, #04-01
Singapore 349278
Tel: (65) 67412178
Fax: (65) 67412179
inquiries@periplus.com.sg
www.tuttlepublishing.com

Printed in China   2109EP
25 24 23 22 21   10 9 8 7 6 5 4 3 2